MARKETING
TO THE
SOCIAL WEB

How Digital Customer Communities Build Your Business

LARRY WEBER

BICENTENNIAL
1807
WILEY
2007
BICENTENNIAL

John Wiley & Sons, Inc.

Library of Congress Cataloging-in-Publication Data:

Weber, Larry.
  Marketing to the social web : how digital customer communities build your
business / Larry Weber.
    p. cm.
  Includes index.
  ISBN 978-0-470-12417-8 (cloth)
    1. Internet marketing.   2. Social networks—Computer network resources.
  I. Title.
HF5415.1265.W43 2007
658.8'72—dc22

                                                              2007007064

Printed in the United States of America.

10 9 8 7 6 5 4 3

For Hannah, Julia, and Geoffrey
. . . may your lives always be a
"verb thing, not a noun thing"

CONTENTS

PART III
MAKING USE OF THE FOUR ONLINE CONDUIT STRATEGIES

PREFACE

In late 1989, I received a phone call from Michael Dertouzos, the founder and head of MIT's Laboratory for Computer Science. He said he wanted to see me for two reasons; first, to help promote the extraordinary innovations coming out of the lab, and second, to discuss marketing some recent work of a young British researcher who was moving to the lab from a stint at CERN (the Organisation Européenne pour la Recherche Nucléaire) in Switzerland.

A few days later, the larger-than-life Michael and a quiet Tim Berners-Lee were sitting in my Cambridge office. Michael spoke of the lab's many accomplishments and the work in progress. He showed me a videotape of his 1980 appearance on the *Today* show where he discussed the impact of the first personal computers on society. The interviewer pushed Michael to agree that the advent of the PC was just a fad, but Michael politely disagreed and went on to describe a world in which a large digital community would soon be formed by connecting all personal computers so that people could easily communicate, shop, learn—even get advice from physicians on another continent. The interviewer just shook his head and broke for a commercial.

Then it was Tim's turn. He discussed his recent work, the development of a language called html—hypertext markup language—that he planned to layer onto the Internet to create a world wide web. He asked if I thought the name was catchy, and I smiled, because I really had no idea what he was talking about.

Michael explained he was forming the World Wide Web Consortium and he wanted us to help promote and educate the world. Now, some 18 years later, we still have not realized the full impact of this

vii

important innovation of our lifetimes. Michael left us too early, and Bill Gates with whom Michael often consulted on a variety of topics about the future, called his passing a major loss in one of the main news weeklies. Tim, now Sir Tim, continues to work on his next phase, the semantic web, and I heeded Michael's advice to study the marketing implications of the Web.

The Web has and will continue to change everything. A world of transparent content, mostly user-generated, broadband, rich media, and available on multiple devices, continues to evolve. Marketing at its best is the influencing of opinion through compelling content; doing so through the Web will get harder before it gets easier, but the change is gaining momentum. The Web has consumed almost all the traditional media: television, print, radio, and direct mail and will make marketing a set of dialogues. Companies will have to learn to contribute to these dialogues and share with their customers and potential customers. I've written this book to suggest how you can do just that.

LARRY WEBER
Buenos Aires, Summer 2007

ACKNOWLEDGMENTS

irst and foremost I must thank my phenomenal cowriter Wally Wood, who truly understood my goals, thinking, and organization around this important book, as well as our earlier book, *The Provocateur*. These books would not have happened without his skillful hand. Thanks to Marijean Lauzier for always supporting my visionary discretions. Jackie Lustig, Jan Baxter, Cinny Little, and all at W2 Group who gave freely of their time and talents to bring this book to fruition while making my "second" career such a joy.

Reid Hoffman (LinkedIn.com), Diane Hessan (Communispace), John Palfrey (Berkman Center for Internet & Society), Tom Gerace (Gather.com), Don McLagan (Compete.com), Dan Morrison (ITtoolbox .com), Josh Scribner (IBM Corporate Communications), Halley Suitt, Stuart Brotman (American Television Experience), Jerry Swerling (Annenberg School for Communication at USCLA), and Judy Strauss (UofN, Reno) all gave of their time but, more importantly, their deepest thinking on the social web. I am forever indebted to them, as I am to the many clients and former clients, the large group of academics, authors, politicians, and executives who freely engaged in numerous conversations that helped shape my thinking.

I thank my agent Jill Kneerim and my editor Richard Narramore whose subtle but swift and clear touch has made this book a very good read. Also, thanks to all the great people at Wiley including Tiffany Groglio and Micheline Frederick, who made the process of producing this book as painless as possible.

Finally, and as always, I want to thank my family, especially Dawn, for supporting and loving a dreamer businessman who wants to help good businesses become great.

Pandemonium: The Landscape of the Social Web

CHAPTER 1

The Web Is Not a Channel

(And You're an Aggregator, Not a Broadcaster)

L earning to market to the social web requires learning a new way to communicate with an audience in a digital environment. It's that simple.

It does not require executives to forget everything they know about marketing. It does mean that they have to open their minds to new possibilities, social change, and rethinking past practices. In the pages ahead, I look at what we can learn about these new possibilities and what the *social web* is about.

Instead of continuing as broadcasters, marketers should—will— become aggregators of customer communities. Rather than broadcasting marketing messages to an increasingly indifferent, even resentful, audience jaded by the 2,000-plus messages the average American is reputedly exposed to every day, marketers should participate in, organize, and encourage social networks to which people want to belong. Rather than talking *at* customers, marketers should talk *with* them. And the social web is the most effective way in the history of the world to do just that on a large scale.

The social web is the online place where people with a common interest can gather to share thoughts, comments, and opinions. It includes social networks such as MySpace, Gather, Friendster, Facebook, BlackPlanet, Eons, LinkedIn, and hundreds more. It includes branded web destinations like Amazon, Netflix, and eBay. It includes enterprise sites such as IBM, Circuit City, Cisco, and Oracle. The social web is a new world of unpaid media created by individuals or enterprises on the Web. These new strategies, which have the capacity to change public opinion every hour—if not every minute—include:

- *Reputation aggregators* are search engines such as Google, Yahoo, Ask, and Microsoft's new Live. They aggregate sites with the best product or service to offer and usually put things in order of reputation.

- *Blogs* (a contraction of *web logs*) are online journals where people can post ideas, images, and links to other web pages or sites.

- *E-communities* are generally advertising supported although some are free; they focus on professional media such as trade magazines. Examples include BusinessWeek.com, SmartMoney.com, and FastCompany.com. Less well-known e-communities include MediaPost.com, ASJA.org, and allrecipes.com.

- *Social networks* are places where people with a common interest or concern come together to meet people with similar interests, express themselves, and vent. In addition to the examples I've already cited, there's iVillage, Xanga, Stumbleupon, MedNetwork, and Flickr.

In traditional publisher- or corporate-controlled media such as newspapers, magazines, radio, and television, the communication is overwhelmingly one way. Professional journalists research and write stories that are edited and disseminated to the public.

Social media such as blogs, however, allow everyone to publish and to participate in multithreaded conversations online. Because bloggers, sometimes referred to as "citizen journalists," have no editorial constraints and have access to the entire Web, their posts can make or break personal, product, or corporate reputations.

Online communities started in the early days of the Internet; software companies encouraged "user groups" to test and experiment with new programs. The Well in California, CompuServe, and America Online built on that idea and began to attract people to the Internet who didn't have a community or who felt somewhat on the fringe of the new social order, where the groups were a way to meet and bond with new people. As Reid Hoffman, the founder of LinkedIn.com, says, "It was almost like the frontier. Who were the people who originally went West? They felt they don't really fit with this society; were somewhat alienated; and wanted to take a big risk. So they got in their wagons and headed West to make something happen. That's the reason why there was this fascination with things like chat rooms and message boards. Wow, you are with these people you don't know. Anonymity was a big part of this because it was like this Wild West kind of community."

Today, there are online tools to manage and present your identity, to communicate with people, to bring yourself online and make yourself heard. Today, individuals and organizations are founding Web-based communities at a mind-boggling pace. People are using the Web to find others with similar interests, to shop more efficiently, to learn about products and services, to vent about shoddy products and poor service, and to stay in touch with distant relatives and friends on the other side of the world.

As Microsoft CEO Steven A. Ballmer told the *New York Times* during a recent discussion about the future of software, "I think one pervasive change is the increasing importance of community. That will come in different forms, with different age groups of people, and it will change as the technology evolves. But the notion of multiple people interacting on things—that will forever continue. That's different today, and we're going to see those differences build. You see it in a variety of ways now, in social networking sites, in the way people collaborate at work, and in ad hoc collaboration over the Internet. You see it in things like Xbox Live, the way we let people come together and have community entertainment experiences. And you'll see that in TV and video. It's not like the future of entertainment has been determined. But it's a big deal."[1]

Here's an example of social media at work: Not long ago, Gillette became concerned that the scruffy, unshaven look was becoming popular among young men. While the look went back to Don Johnson and George Michael, it seemed to be spreading through fashion ads, men's magazines, and television actors. Clearly, Gillette's shaver business suffers when men shave less.

Gillette and its advertising agency, Digitas, came up with a campaign to influence behavior change in men. They created a video that looked as if someone had recorded a television news report of women around the world demonstrating against unshaven men and put it on YouTube. They also established a website, noscruf.com, which purports to be the home of the National Organization of Social Crusaders Repulsed by Unshaven Faces, with the motto, "Let's end the trend of prickly, scratchy, stubbly faces. We're not going to shave until men do." There is a picture of bikini-clad "Terry Tarentelli, swimsuit model and NoScruf Founder," with hirsute armpits and legs.

The site offers visitors a short movie, "In Your Dreams, Stubble Boy," in which the unshaven hero's girlfriend asks him to consider a world in which women stop shaving and withhold sex until men change their ways. Site visitors can forward the film, e-mail their feelings about stubble to unshaven friends, and join the movement.

What the site does not show is any connection to Gillette or Digitas. Nor has the corporation run ads for NoScruf.org; visitors have had to find it either via YouTube or through friends. Within six weeks of launch, more than a million people had found the site. Six months later, the counter at the bottom of the site showed over 12 million visitors. "We'll see campaigns like this more and more as people spend time online," says Wendi Smith, a spokeswoman for Gillette. "You have to earn the attention of consumers here more than any other medium, partly because we're accustomed to surfing and it's easy to click away. Also, consumers are not necessarily going to go directly to a marketer's site, therefore we need to do something entertaining to grab them. In the beginning of a campaign, launching unbranded can spark interest and engage consumers."[2]

Did the site sell a single razor for Gillette? I suspect no one knows (and Gillette certainly isn't talking). Did it change the attitudes of some young men and women about the scruffy look? Probably. With 70 percent of the razor market, anything that encourages men—and women—to shave helps Gillette. This is just one example of marketing to the social web. It's a harbinger of your future.

Pandemonium in Media and Markets

As Gillette's managers know, the marketing worlds are pandemonium these days. American consumers have more choices, more products, more services, more media, more messages, and more digital conversations than ever. Consider media:

- *Television.* Between cable and satellite, the average American household receives 70 or more television stations, a number that continues to grow, and the average time spent viewing continues to hold its own. Because some news viewers are migrating to the Internet, NBC Universal recently announced that it intended to reduce its newsgathering staff by 5 percent, or 300 people—and perhaps much more to offset advertising losses from its prime-time schedule.

- *Magazines.* Although publishers introduced more than 1,000 new magazine titles last year, the total number of titles, average magazine circulation, and single-copy sales continue to drift downward.

- *Newspapers.* Newspaper circulation has been falling, a plunge hastened by the Web, and advertising is following readers out the door. Classified ads are shifting online to sites like Monster.com (jobs) and Craigslist.com (jobs and everything else). And while newspapers have not yet begun to shut down in large numbers, it is only a matter of time. Newspaper jobs are already disappearing. According to the Newspaper Association of America, the number of people employed in the industry fell by 18 percent between 1990 and 2004.

- *Radio.* Sirius satellite radio now offers 55 channels of sports, news, and commentary and 69 channels of commercial-free music. XM Satellite Radio, which may have merged with Sirius by the time you read this, offers 150 channels of commercial-free music. You don't want to listen to commercials? Subscribe to satellite radio.

New product marketing is also pandemonium, for example:

- According to the Food Institute, marketers introduced over 16,000 new food products last year (over 2,500 new beverages alone). They introduced over 13,000 nonfood products—including 4,230 new cosmetics, 2,793 new skin care items, and 1,259 new hair care products.
- Exhibitors at the International Consumer Electronics Show introduced more than 10,000 new audio, digital imaging/video, gaming, home theater, home networking, mobile, and wireless products.
- Exhibitors at the International Home and Housewares Show introduced another 10,000-plus new small kitchen appliances, kitchenware, bath and shower accessories, decorative accessories, and personal care appliances.
- Exhibitors at the National Hardware Show introduced another 5,000-plus new hardware, home, and garden items.
- The list goes on: Exhibitors at the New York Auto Show introduced . . . Exhibitors at the Ft. Lauderdale International Boat Show . . . Exhibitors at the International Camping and Outdoor Show . . . but you get the idea—and this does not include business-to-business products and services. Or new pharmaceuticals and medical devices. Or travel opportunities . . . or educational offerings.

What's a marketer to do in this teeming mass of newnesses?

From Broadcasters to Aggregators

Before looking ahead, let's take a quick look back. Not so very long ago, marketers got the word out about their products or services in any way they could—newspaper and magazine ads, billboards, radio and television commercials. Each new medium added something. Magazines added color and national distribution to newspaper advertising. Billboards were in your face as you drove along the highways. Radio added sound and music. Television added movement and, even more than billboards or radio, intrusiveness.

Remember the days when the marketer controlled the message? About all television viewers could do was watch or change channels (or go to the toilet), and for a good long time television advertising was incredibly effective. It still is for many products in many situations, but its very success brought about consumer reaction.

Today, 90 percent of the people who can avoid TV ads through TiVo, DVD recording, or the skip button on the VCR remote do so. In fact, only 18 percent of television advertising campaigns actually generate a positive return on the investment. And although total TV viewership has remained steady, new channels have fragmented the audience to such an extent that the broadcast networks NBC, CBS, and ABC have all lost audiences both relatively and absolutely.

Despite their shrinking audiences, these networks and other TV channels continue to raise their ad rates; the cost per thousand (CPM) people reached by the average television commercial increased 265 percent between 1996 and 2005. Television advertisers are not happy, and some big ones—Procter & Gamble, American Express, McDonald's—have begun experimenting with alternatives, but no major advertiser has decided to do something else.

It won't be news to you that most advertising is incredibly inefficient. When you advertise in mass media, you generally reach far more people than the potential customers you intend to reach. But as long as the CPMs were small, who cared? A certain amount of advertising waste was a cost of doing business.

True, marketers have tried to improve their advertising's efficiency. They've tried to match audience demographics—age, sex, education, income, household size—to their target market. For example, beer commercials appear in sports programs that young men tend to watch and disposable diaper commercials in daytime dramas that young mothers often watch. Still, demographics don't really work very well in trying to identify a target market for most products. Middle-aged and older men drink beer; fathers buy disposable diapers.

For 150 years or more, marketers, through newspapers, magazines, and then radio and television, have been broadcasting their messages to a potential market that they defined as well as they could. Advertisers have tried to put their ads in front of those prospective customers most likely to buy the company's product or service. But the goal has always been to reach as many people as possible with the hope that enough paying customers would respond to make the investment pay.

Today, sophisticated marketers realize that what worked in the past is not working (or not working well) now—and they need a new approach. As A. G. Lafley, the CEO of Procter & Gamble, told his executives, "We need to reinvent the way we market to consumers. We need a new model."

The Web Is Not a Channel

Steve Ballmer's observation hints at how thoroughly the social web will change our world. A century ago, although no one knew it at the time, the first automobile was not simply a self-propelled buggy. True, it got you from one place to another, but it also changed the face of the country, the design of cities. It changed courting behavior and where people could live and work. Similarly, television was not simply radio with pictures. By showing ordinary people in Eastern Europe and in the Soviet Union the lives of ordinary people in the West, television affected history. By showing Americans the Vietnam War in living color, television changed American society.

The Web will have as profound an effect on society as the automobile or television. In fact, we're only beginning to glimpse the Web's implications. For instance, the Web undoes some of the effects of 50 years of television. Remember how, in the early days of television, the ads and many programs showed the happy family—dad, mom, son, and sister—sitting together in front of the living room television? Today the reality is more like dad, mom, son, and sister all watching their own sets in separate rooms. Rather than bringing people together, television has, in many senses, brought about more isolation. People are home alone even if others are in the house; it is easier to click on the TV than go out to a bowling league, lodge night, or card game with the girls. In contrast, the social web, through the dialogue it encourages, is beginning to bring people together.

Since the dawn of the television age, the message of virtually all commercials has been: Buy! Buy! Buy! The unspoken contract was: Somebody's got to pay for your news, entertainment, diversion and that's advertising, so Buy! Buy! Buy Now! Broadly speaking, for the past 60 years, most marketers have debated how to use television, radio, print, public relations, direct marketing, the Internet, customer retention programs. What is the best medium to reach our market? What are our customers reading, watching, listening to? How can we attract their attention, stop them from turning the page or changing the channel? How can we best tell them about our product, our service, our benefits, our value?

For the past 10 years, corporations have been trained that they should use all the different media—newspapers, magazines, direct mail, television, public relations, and then the Internet. But the Internet is becoming the umbrella. Managers have to understand that the Web is rapidly becoming the most important marketing medium. If you are a corporate marketer, you don't just drop some ads onto websites the way you have dropped 30 spots into television shows or a color spread into a magazine. A symptom of how things are changing: almost two-thirds of the commercials during last year's Super Bowl were designed to send viewers to a digital destination.

But as you've noticed, people don't want to be sold. They are doing their best to avoid commercials. They have pop-up blockers to screen out the ads on the Web that are a distraction. Early Web advertisers, who saw the medium as just another advertising channel, treated it like a magazine ad equipped with sound and motion. But banner ads and pop-ups are not the best way to market on the Web.

What people do want is news and information about the things they care about. They want to be able to find out about the things they care about right now. One recent midnight, a friend's dog tangled with a skunk for the first time. She had no tomato juice, the traditional folk bath for a skunked dog. Five minutes on the Web, however, and she'd found a formula that included hydrogen peroxide and liquid dish detergent that she could mix up and de-stink the dog.

Community building—with communities focusing on a specific common interest—is one of the fastest growing applications on the Web. Examples include: ITtoolbox.com, where information technology professionals swap opinions on technology products and services; BootsnAll.com, where budget travelers share advice about, say, the best hotels in Katmandu; iVillage.com, where women trade ideas about diet and fitness, love and sex, home and food; HealthBoards.com, which has subgroups on 140 diseases that serve as forums for people to share experiences and discuss problems or new discoveries; and LinkedIn.com, where professionals go to network. All of this means that the Web is continuing to evolve.

Four Generations of the Web

During the first phase of the Web, 1990 to 1995, the focus was HTML and site building. I was present at the beginning. My experience with the Internet began in 1989 to 1990 when Michael Dertouzos, then the director of MIT's Laboratory for Computer Science, asked me to help promote the lab. It had developed a number of groundbreaking technologies—from RSA security to the spreadsheet to Ethernet—and Michael had successfully recruited Tim Berners-Lee to work on HTML at MIT. I helped lead the announcement of the World Wide Web Consortium based on the development of HTML.

We did early work for America Online (AOL), helping them establish and market early communities, then called chat rooms. The popular ones were for breast cancer survivors, Boston Red Sox fans, and personal finance. We helped Monster.com build its community, and in the mid-1990s, we launched E-GM for General Motors, one of the first automotive communities.

I've been deeply involved in many software and technology companies over the past 25 years such as Verizon Wireless, Hewlett Packard, Lotus Development, and RedHat. I helped found the largest interactive trade group in the country, Massachusetts Innovation and Technology Exchange, which is now 11 years old, with over 3,000 members. And during this time, I've watched the Internet evolve.

With the advent of the browser, the second phase involved more interactivity and transactional things, search, click-throughs, and pop-ups. That phase lasted almost 10 years and has now given way to the third phase: the rise of the social web, all the things I have been describing and will be talking about in detail in the chapters ahead.

Web 4.0, which is right around the corner, will feature rich media (full of video, sound, even touch) and broadband, with high definition making the Web more emotive. How does this work? Consider the growing popularity of video conferencing. For instance, at a Halo center, where the next generation of video-conferencing technology is in place, participants see three-dimensional, full-size, video conferencing; it's almost as if the people are in the same room and sharing the same experience. That is an example of rich media in action. The emotive element will include both personal and business sensations, the idea that the experiences offer not only emotions—joy, curiosity, disgust, happiness—but also, on the business side, sensations of satisfaction and fulfillment.

In this new world, the customer is in control. There are still only 24 hours a day, and if people become more involved with the Web, they're not going to have as much time to watch television, they're not going to listen to the radio, and they're not going to read the newspaper or a magazine. Publishers know this and are doing their best to create websites that can supplement (or replace) their paper publications.

The real job of the marketer in the social web is to aggregate customers. You aggregate customers two ways: (1) by providing compelling content on your website and creating retail environments that customers want to visit and (2) by going out and participating in the public arena. If you are in the energy business, you should be participating in the energy blogosphere. If you are a pharmaceutical manufacturer, you should be participating in discussions about disease and its treatment. If you are a small fly rod maker, you should be participating in discussions about fly fishing.

Note that you do not have to be a *Fortune* 500 corporation to participate in these conversations. Indeed, it may be easier and more effective for a relatively small or medium-size company to take maximum advantage of the principles I lay out in this book.

The social web will be the most critical marketing environment around. Much the way newspapers were critical in the 1800s, magazines and radio were critical in the first half of the twentieth century, and television was critical in the second half, the Internet began to become significant in the 1990s. It is rapidly growing more and more critical to marketing, but has shifted into a social digital space that I am calling the social web.

The social web will become the primary center of activity for whatever you do when you shop, plan, learn, or communicate. It may not take over your entire life (one hopes), but it will be the first place you turn for news, information, entertainment, diversion—all of the things that the older media supplied.

Marketing, therefore, has to wrap around that—because what is truly changing in the social web is media and marketing has always had to shape itself around media. So individuals are becoming media, as are companies. As you produce content, you become a medium.

How do you now market in this new environment? Ultimately, marketing disappears if it does its job right, because marketers become purveyors of environment. A manager of an environment helps people make decisions to buy. That is the commercial and modernization side of things. A good example is how the brilliant chairman of Starbucks, Howard Schultz, and his people keep thinking about how they can enrich the Starbucks environment without turning people away. They've brought in music . . . some social causes . . . and Wi-Fi. Now think about how you can create digital experiences that encourage your customers to come back for more. There is pandemonium around the social web, like anything in its first phases, but it will self-organize.

It is important to understand that although we are at the beginning of the social web, marketers should dive in *now*. If you wait much longer, your competitors will have figured out how to attract your customers to their environments. If that happens, you will have to work three times as hard to get them back. Customers have only so much time. And if they're happy where they are, then they're less likely to leave.

A business friend started and runs a large retail clothing chain. When I saw him not long ago and asked how thing were going, he told me, "Well, good. My core loyal customers of the past 20 years are still core loyal customers. But when I go into the stores, I notice they're all starting to look older. Where are the younger people?" I suggested that they might be on SmartBargains.com or another clothing site. My friend had never heard of it.

Unless there's a change, my friend's chain will reach the proverbial tipping point; suddenly there are no customers in the stores. If that chain (or any retailer) does not get involved in social media and marketing, it will lose a whole generation of customers. They simply won't come to stores. They want a dialogue with your business, want to know you are there and available 24/7. The idea of branding in the social web is the dialogue you have with your customer. The stronger the dialogue, the stronger your brand; the weaker the dialogue, the weaker your brand. You can easily find examples of great brands that have lost their dialogue: Sony, Disney, Coke, McDonald's. Worse, was Wal-Mart's effort to co-opt the blogosphere.

A blog called Wal-Marting Across America featured the adventures of Jim (a photographer) and Laura (a writer), no last names, as they traveled from Las Vegas to Georgia in an RV, parking overnight in Wal-Mart parking lots. "Every Wal-Mart employee that Laura and Jim run into, from store clerks to photogenic executives, absolutely loves to work at the store," reported *BusinessWeek*. The upbeat stories seemed too good to be true to critics of Wal-Mart, and in a sense the critics were right.

Jim is a photographer for the *Washington Post,* and Laura, his girl-friend, is a U.S. Treasury employee who does freelance writing on the side. It was their idea to rent an RV and park free at Wal-Mart stores.

However, when Laura talked to her brother, a publicist whose firm represents Working Families for Wal-Mart, the advocacy group offered to fly Jim and Laura to Las Vegas, rent the RV, and pay for the gas, set up the blog, and pay Laura a freelance fee for her entries.

Once bloggers heard that Jim and Laura were, in effect, working for Wal-Mart (which supports Working Families for Wal-Mart), they were furious. Although Jim and Laura felt they'd done nothing wrong—"We were planning a trip on our own dime, and we were thrilled to have a sponsor who would do all our legwork," said Laura—others were more critical. The *Washington Post*'s executive editor made it clear that Jim's involvement violated internal ethics guidelines, and Jim had to pay back $2,200 received for the trip and remove his photographs from the blog. Commenting on the debacle, Paul Rand, a partner at Ketchum public relations, "Today, there's nowhere to run and nowhere to hide. The moment you hide something, you will end up being exposed and picked apart."[3] I see this as an example of a giant brand—Wal-Mart—trying to figure out the social web and doing it wrong.

McDonald's is trying to gain the dialogue back. Its sites are becoming very social in nature, especially focused around nutrition. And the company is now offering coffee from Newman's Own—a company with a social conscience that McDonald's hopes is going to rub off. This is not a small consideration. The concept of moral purpose in branding is going to come to life in the social web.

By moral purpose, I mean offering value and acting ethically and transparently. No business will succeed without a clear definition of its transparency in doing business. The ethics around doing business include: environmental responsibility, diversity in employment, considering the larger effect of the company's actions. In other words, you need to have moral purpose embedded in your values, along with great products at a great price. The real issue is to learn how to market on the social web responsibly. But first, let me talk a little more about what the social web means to marketers.

"Customers are screaming to be more engaged with the companies that affect their lives," is how Diane Hessan describes the change. As president and CEO of Communispace, which builds and runs private online customer communities, Diane sees unmistakable signs that the social web is part of that change. "Booming trends like blogging, on-line communities, flash mobbing, buzz agents, and MySpace show that customers have a lot to say—they want to be asked and they want to be involved." If you haven't already heard about flash mobbing and buzz agents, you soon will. Flash mobbing is assembling a group of people via the Internet or other digital communications networks; they suddenly appear in a public place, do something unusual for a brief time, and then disperse. Buzz agents are paid shills; they talk up the product or service without identifying their connection to the company.

For a glimpse at the social web's influence on the role of marketing, consider GlaxoSmithKline's experience with Communispace. In preparation for the launch of its first weight reduction product, Glaxo sponsored an online weight loss community. This was a real win-win. The members benefited by meeting other women who supported their dieting struggles through instant messaging and chat discussions. Glaxo benefited as the members answered questions about product packaging, offered advice on where to place the product in stores, and, most significantly, discussed their battles with the scale.

These community discussions helped shape Glaxo's advertising and packaging for the company's diet pill. They also uncovered rampant confusion about dieting. As *BusinessWeek* reported, "In one exchange, a member stated that you could lose weight by drinking eight glasses of water a day, while another said no, it's eight quarts. A third added that the water doesn't count if it's in coffee, but this person was quickly contradicted."

Over time, community members come to trust one another even though they may be scattered all over the country, and their responses can be quite revealing. When Glaxo asked the group to use images that showed how they felt about themselves, the women posted photos of hippos and elephants. Says Andrea Harkins, senior research manager at GlaxoSmithKline Consumer Healthcare: "These are things they wouldn't have said in words."

In the end, the online community gave Glaxo far more information than it could have obtained from focus groups. As an additional
benefit, the community has created an intensely enthusiastic corps of
product evangelists. One member said about Glaxo, "They have done
an incredible job of reaching out into the community and giving us all
hope that someone out there cares about us and we are not alone in
our struggle to lose weight."[1] The marketer's new job is to build communities of interest and provide content. The reason to do so—as the
rest of this book will demonstrate—is to cut the marketing budget and
reach more people more effectively.

Who's Really in Control Here?

The goal of marketing has always been and will continue to be
building and leveraging relationships between your organization and
various customers—current and prospective consumers of your
products and services plus employees, partners, shareholders, government, the media, analysts, and all the rest. Obviously, strong relationships are crucial to establishing and extending brand value,
strengthening and protecting corporate and product reputation, and
boosting demand. But you have to do all this while under constant
pressure to improve marketing's return on investment in a highly
competitive global economy.

As I suggested in Chapter 1, marketing's traditional tools for getting the word out are growing rusty. Not only are fewer Americans
watching broadcast television in both absolute and relative terms,
they're avoiding the commercials with the remote, TiVO, and 30-
second skip function on their videocassette recorders. They're avoiding
telemarketers through the National Do Not Call Registry, avoiding Internet pop-up and banner ads through software programs, avoiding
radio commercials through the iPod and other digital music devices,
and avoiding print ads the way they always did—by turning the page.

As a result, the job of national advertisers is more complicated
than ever; it's more work and expense to run ads in several places than
it is to deal with one major magazine or three dominant television

networks. For smaller advertisers, the changes have meant they can afford targeted vehicles in which to advertise. But for most advertisers, the growth of vehicles has meant that their advertising becomes more efficient—if they can define their target market well, they can probably find a vehicle that reaches that target market. It is the difference between advertising Titleist clubs in *Time* and in *Golf Digest*.

The control of information, however, continues to shift from marketers to consumers. The explosion of media choice has undermined the mass marketing model because it is dramatically harder to put together a mass audience than it was when everyone you wanted to reach was watching just three television networks. Today, the computer, the Internet, and broadband access allow consumers to find what they want when they want it. You're not in control any more.

Consumers love control so much that when they hear about devices like TiVo and the DVRs they want them mainly for the control they offer. They can watch a program when they want, not when it conflicts with a child's music lesson or a client meeting. Apple's iPod and its competitors have profited from this attitude. Once people get used to the idea that they can have their news and weather when they want them and how they want them, and they can have their television when they want it and how they want it, they wonder, "Why can't I have my music when I want it—without commercials?"

Forrester Research did a study not long ago that investigated consumer rejection of advertising. The researchers asked about consumers' level of interest in things like digital video recorders and ad blocking software. They also asked about interest in a device that would record and play radio content while automatically rejecting commercials—basically a TiVo for radio, although no such thing existed. Consumers were just as interested in the nonexistent radio recorder as they were in the television recorder. All they had to do was hear about it—a new way to take control!—and they wanted it.

Consumers now have access to devices to control their choice of entertainment, news, information, and diversions, so there's no going back to the days when a deep-pocketed advertiser could buy the same time on all three television networks and set up a roadblock to overcome channel switching. People who want to watch *Lost* or *Stargate* without commercials will have to wait for the DVD. Or, more and more, they can download the episode for a small fee. This may be good for the people who own the shows, but it's not so good if you're a marketer who sees *Lost* or *Stargate* viewers as your target audience.

Think your company (or any company) has any control over what consumers hear, see, watch, read, or do these days? In my experience, you actually have less control than ever. True, old habits die hard and company personalities change glacially. As consumers are doing their best to avoid commercial messages, some marketers are dreaming up ways to slip past their defenses. Thus, consumers are served up commercials before movie showings; blatant product placement in video games, movies, and television shows like *American Idol*; and commercials on in-store and airport television networks. Even the bathroom is no refuge: consider the "Wizmark," which, sensitive to very slight motion, will light up, play music, and deliver an advertising pitch from within a men's urinal to a briefly captive audience of one.

The techniques du jour are viral marketing, buzz marketing, word-of-mouth marketing, or stealth marketing—the idea that a company can hire people to pretend to be consumers to recommend a product or service. A liquor company might hire attractive young women to visit crowded bars, order the advertiser's product, then turn to the next person and say, "This is really delicious; you ought to try one of these."

Sony Ericsson hired actors to pretend to be tourists who asked strangers to snap their picture. What the "tourists" handed over was not a camera but a new combination cell phone and digital camera. They were trading on people's willingness to do a kindness to expose them to the product. "We wanted to find a way of actually touching people," said Nicky Csellak-Claeys, head of strategic marketing for Sony Ericsson North America. "We take the product to the street and demonstrate how it will be used on site."

I think this is a terrible idea, as bad as Wal-Mart's sponsoring a "Wal-Marting Across America" blog. The harm it does to a company's reputation when the deception is revealed (which happens sooner than ever on the Web these days) cannot be offset by any short-term gain in sales or publicity. Marketing has to be both honest and transparent; consumers are cynical enough now—and they are hypersensitive to corporate misbehavior.

We've had 200-plus years of supply-side economy and now we are oversupplied. In an oversupplied world, you have to connect consumers to your products and services. To earn loyalty, you have to build and nurture your customer communities.

Marketers therefore have two daunting challenges. First, you have to justify your spending and your budget through better performance measurement. The pressure is on from senior management to be much more transparent about marketing investments and the return on those investments. Second, you must connect with customers and prospects who are increasingly harder to reach. How do you deliver a message that resonates with customers and induces them to buy what you're selling?

The objective is to have customers invite you to deliver the message to them. You just can't force it on them any more.

Marketing's Role Has Changed

As I've already suggested, the explosive growth of the social web has changed the marketer's role from a *broadcaster* pushing out messages and materials to an *aggregator* who brings together content, enables collaboration, and builds and participates in communities. As an aggregator, you bring together content, collaborate with your customers, and engage your online communities. Content includes new ideas, research, and opinions. Collaboration creates an open environment in which people can, and do, share knowledge. The aggregator extends invitations to individuals as well as to groups to join communities of interest.

Most stories about the social web focus on the "cool" aspects, such as YouTube.com (everyone can be a movie actor/director/producer), MySpace.com (talk to friends, meet people, network with coworkers), or SecondLife.com (a 3-D virtual world entirely built and owned by its more than 1.1 million residents). Despite all the chatter, there is a strong business case for integrating the social web into your marketing toolkit. The social web provides numerous opportunities for strengthening and expanding relationships with all your customers. These opportunities include:

- *Targeted brand building.* Depending on the size and breadth of a company's customer base, communities can be organized by vertical market (e.g., high tech, energy, consumer packaged goods, retail, automotive) or by horizontal topics that cut across multiple sectors (e.g., finance, manufacturing, the environment). To build your organization's brand, consider hosting a podcast—an online audio that users can download to a device such as an iPod—on a hot topic such as change management, outsourcing, risk management, corporate governance, innovation, or talent management. Sessions could be moderated by an analyst or a journalist and feature customers sharing their experiences with their peers. Senior executive blogs and microsites (websites developed with a particular focus for a specific target audience) can help establish industry thought leadership.

- *Lead generation.* At launch time, you can introduce the new product or service both in the online and offline worlds. Using the Web, you can reach more people—and reach highly targeted markets—more quickly and more cost-effectively than through traditional broadcast and print media. You can stimulate lead generation by, say, offering a white paper in return for having people register on your site and give you some basic information. You can encourage product trials through online demonstrations. You can attract prospective customers to online contests.

- *Partnerships.* In addition to customers and prospects, the social web is a great tool for staying connected with distributors, technology vendors, manufacturers, and other business partners. Often companies announce these partnerships with great fanfare but they fade away over time because it requires a significant effort to maintain them. An e-community or social network can help your company's distributors, store managers, sales representatives, and others stay in touch and consult with one another. A community is a flexible platform for your partners to receive the latest company updates, news from the head office, and stories from the field.

- *Research and development.* Isolation is the greatest obstacle to product and service innovation. Conversely, collaboration stimulates new ideas and new approaches that can lead to breakthrough solutions to complex problems. Blogs, wikis (websites that allow users to add, remove, or edit content easily), online communities, and social networks can be used to bring product developers together in real time. Scientists can get immediate feedback on their research, make corrections and move on to the next challenge. Some businesses have built private online communities to obtain consumer input on new products during development. As GlaxoSmithKline learned, by including customers in the product development process, companies can forge bonds that foster long-term product or brand loyalty.

- *Employee communications.* The social web tools also afford numerous opportunities to strengthen and expand employee communications. For example, internal webcasts—using streaming media technology to take a single content source and distribute it to many listeners/viewers at one time—can provide employees with updates on specific topics such as new accounting rules or new product features. You can distribute company news or human resource benefits information to mobile devices as a way to stay in touch with employees who travel extensively or spend most of their time at client sites. You can create private online forums where salespeople share experiences and ask each other for advice. If you're looking for new talent, you can tap into business or career networks such as LinkedIn.com or Vault.com to identify and reach prospective employees.

All of these strategies incorporate significant enterprise-generated content. In the social media world, material that traditionally has appeared in published form—ads, press releases, brochures, articles, white papers, and the like—is generated to facilitate participation and interaction. For example, Pontiac announced that it was setting up a 96-acre Motorati Island in the Second Life virtual world (and paying about $7,500 in actual dollars to Linden Lab, Second Life's creator). Pontiac will sell virtual versions of its Solstice GXP car to the world's virtual residents and stage virtual races on a track it will build on the virtual island.

"Right now there isn't a car culture in Second Life, but we know there's a huge car culture with human beings," said Tor Myhren, executive creative director at Leo Burnett, Pontiac's ad agency. "Certainly there's going to be one there and we want to be part of it." Myhren said Pontiac hopes to fit into the Second Life culture by using its island to showcase resident creations rather than simply display the brand. Residents will be allowed to customize the cars any way they like. "We're trying to go far beyond a press release saying we're on Second Life. We want to connect with the people there."[2]

Opportunities to Achieve Community

How can you and your company get involved? You can either join in other people's communities or create your own destinations and invite others to join in the conversation there. Or you can do both.

Pontiac, for example, is joining the Second Life conversation. Depending on your marketing goal, it is possible to join all kinds of conversations both as an organization and as an individual within the organization. The advantage of joining another organization's community, like FaceBook or YouTube, is that it already has members who come to it regularly. On the other hand, you may not be able to find the exact community you need, so you have to create your own.

Here's a good example from the publishing world. *Technology Review*, published by a media firm owned by the Massachusetts Institute of Technology, was looking to bring more visitors to its website (technologyreview.com) and boost paid subscriptions. The magazine targets technology and business leaders—CEOs, entrepreneurs, researchers, venture capitalists, and financiers—who are interested in the commercial, social, and political impact of emerging technologies like disease treatment, biotech, energy, and computers.

Although its print editions, website, newsletters, and live events were already attracting more than two million industry and R&D leaders worldwide, the magazine saw opportunities to expand even further through its online presence.

The editors began by searching the Web and observing competitors and influencers in the fields in which it actively participated. Once they had identified the most important and influential individuals who read and responded to the magazine's articles, they began to offer exclusive content tailored to this audience's special interests—brief snippets of articles that would be appearing in the next issue of the magazine. This gave these influential readers both a head start in learning about new research and provided an inducement to read the entire article.

The magazine also began to participate in influencer communities and to promote the *Technology Review* website content. In addition, it used content syndication and e-marketing tactics to increase revenue, gain more audience data, and expand product offerings to advertisers.

As a result, the website attracted more than 100,000 unique visitors during the first two weeks of the campaign. Both the magazine's readership and circulation began to grow—growth that continues to this day. And more than 52 percent of current website traffic is a result of the communities that learned about *Technology Review* from its campaign.

Another example: SAP, the software company, wanted to emphasize a specialized area of expertise in communications with its customers. To do so, SAP created a microsite (as a special area on the main website) around a business problem common to many of the corporation's prospects and customers. SAP posts interesting content and offers ways for customers to talk among themselves, if they want to do so. Also it couples this site with an outbound campaign to the spheres of influence, the communities most interested in hearing about what the company has done and invite them to come to the site to learn more about this particular solution.

This is not much beyond Marketing 101. You must know what business result you're trying to achieve, use relevant traditional marketing tactics and strategies that have proven effective, and then get a little help to leverage some of the new tools that are available today.

New Rules of Engagement

Bear in mind that the social media world is very different from a traditional communications environment. In the traditional communications model, your organization controls content creation and distribution. In the social media world, you have little to no control over content and distribution. Individuals communicate with other individuals and with groups, and groups communicate with individuals and groups—everyone with everyone. It's highly democratic: Everyone has access and everyone can participate. As a marketer, you go to other people's "parties" as well as create your own destinations for other people to come to you.

So what happens, for example, when employees start blogging? Are there rules? Is profanity or character defamation (which may appear in some blogs) going to be permitted? How openly can employees discuss product development? What is considered company confidential information and what is open to the public? Organizations need to establish rules that guide people and help them use the social web tools safely and confidently. I'll be talking about rules in Chapter 14 about blogging.

When you think about rules for participating in the social web, you also face larger issues for corporate governance, especially in terms of promoting accountability, fairness, and transparency. How accountable is the organization for what an employee says in a blog? What kind of comments are "fair" or "unfair"? What does transparency mean when an employee participates in an online community? Is there an obligation to disclose company affiliation? Can employees have a private life on the Web? If you establish clear policies at the outset, you'll save time and aggravation when the inevitable crisis occurs.

How you manage organizational change is affected by the move from traditional communications to the social web environment. Your employees need to understand the new approach and the new rules of engagement. Now is the time to arrange extensive training for managers, bloggers, corporate communicators, human resource professionals, Web strategists, and others who will be engaging in the social web activities. Educate your employees about best practices and provide rewards for applying these practices.

There are also new rules for measuring marketing success in a social web context. The new success measures include share of voice, level of engagement, tone of discourse, evidence/quality of community, and cost of market share. How often is your organization being discussed in the blogosphere? Who's doing the talking and how influential are the participants? What are they saying? Are there recurring themes? Is the tone positive, negative, or neutral? Who's listened to the podcast? Who's downloaded the white paper? Are they asking for more information? How many people participated in the online contest and who are they? What was the impact on leads and sales? Some of these measures are quantifiable and others are qualitative.

The Web itself is inherently measurable, a big plus in this era of marketing accountability. At the very least, you can measure where site visitors are coming from (the referring site), which pages they are clicking through, and where they go next without identifying the visitors themselves. You can learn an extraordinary amount but be aware that the costs can be quite high. Therefore, you have to determine the most important metrics needed to attain the best ROI. I'll talk in more detail about ways to measure the social web in Chapter 12.

Finally, how does the social web fit with your company's digital vision? Digital vision is the long-term strategy for the company's entire online presence. How will you use the website (or websites) to support customer relationship management and online service and support— and how will the social web fit into that framework? Social media is not something to bolt onto a website; it should be an integral part of a company's overall online experience.

You already know that the social web can amplify awareness of your brand, product, or service. Incorporating digital channels into a new product or service launch can help you quickly and cost-effectively reach highly targeted prospects. Communities can serve as referral networks: an opinion leader in the community "endorses" a new product and in a flash other members are downloading the free trial and asking for more information.

In fact, the social web can play a valuable role throughout the entire life cycle of product development, market introduction, and market adoption. During the development phase, you might use blogs, wikis, communities, or all three to get feedback on various product features. During market introduction, you can use podcasts and webinars to engage and educate potential customers about the new product's benefits and applications. (A webinar is a seminar conducted over the Web; unlike a webcast, a webinar is designed to be interactive.) As the product begins to sell, you can use the social web for troubleshooting, problem solving, and customer service and support—plus all-important word-of-mouth to build that buzz.

By now, the benefits of marketing to the social web should be apparent—and viewed as essential to an overall marketing strategy. The social web allows you to engage and influence prospects and customers and build trusted relationships over time. It helps you learn what employees, clients, and partners really think about new products, programs, or other initiatives. And all of this is in near real time and for a fraction of the cost of traditional media. But if you build a site to attract a community, will anyone come?

CHAPTER 3

Making the Transition to the Social Web

(First Change Your Marketing Mindset)

The future is here. Remember how national publications, national radio, and national television led to the rise of mass marketing? That was the first period of marketing. The second period—which is just about over—saw the rise of direct marketing through direct mail, telemarketing, and catalogs. This is hardly new news.

Now we're in the third period of marketing, the era of the social web. Your customers (and potential customers) are more in control of what they read, hear, and watch. And not only do they want to talk to other people, they want you—the marketer—to listen to them. It's time to embrace this new reality. But how do you make the transition from the old marketing to the new marketing of the social web?

The first thing you have to do is change your marketing mindset (see Table 3.1). Then you'll be in a good position to change your approach to brand equity, segmentation, targeting, communication, content, virality, reviews, the role of advertisers and publishers, the hierarchy of information, and—inevitably—payment.

This is not just another 12-step program. It's a great way to organize your thinking about the differences between the traditional marketing of yesterday and the new marketing of today and tomorrow, starting with a new mindset.

The New Marketing Mindset

As you saw in the previous chapter, marketing's role has not changed. It's still about defining target markets, communicating with prospective customers, building loyalty, and so on. But the techniques that were successful in the past will be less and less effective in the future. This is where your new marketing mindset comes in.

Clear your mind of all those one-way, one-sided communication techniques, all those ways of spouting only your side of the story. Marketing to the social web is not about you getting *your* story out, it's about your customers. It's about being more transparent, earning trust, building credibility. It's about nurturing relationships and dialogue among customers, prospects, your company, and whoever else is active in the community.

Bring Your Brand Alive

To win the branding war, you have to recognize that brand equity is shifting away from brand essence and brand recall. Those were key elements in the old marketing and resulted in what I call the *stationary* brands, like Kodak, Disney, and Kellogg's.

But a brand is actually a living, changing thing, especially in the new marketing. It is difficult for many marketing people and C-level executives to admit that their brand is a living thing. Yet, in the new marketing reality, the brand is based on the dialogue you have with your customers and prospects—the stronger the dialogue, the stronger the brand; the weaker the dialogue, the weaker the brand.

TABLE 3.1   Old Marketing versus New Marketing

Components	Old Marketing	New Marketing
Marketing mindset	Use one-way, one-sided communication to tell brand story.	Nurture dialogue and relationships; be more transparent, earn trust, build credibility.
Brand equity	Brand recall is holy grail.	Brand value is determined by customers: How likely are customers to highly recommend the good or service?
Segmentation	Group customers by demographics.	Group customers by behavior, attitudes, and interests—what's important to them.
Targeting	Target by demographics, especially for media buying.	Target according to customer behavior.
Communication	Broadcast style: create and push message out for customers to absorb.	Digital environment for interactive communication through search and query, customer comments, personal reviews, or dialogue.
Content	Professional content created and controlled by marketers.	Mix of professional and user-generated content, increasingly visual.
Virality	A nice feature but popularity too often driven by flashy presentation rather than content.	Virality based on solid content about remarkable products or features that will get people talking and forwarding e-mail.

(continued)

TABLE 3.1　(*Continued*)

Components	Old Marketing	New Marketing
Reviews	Think Michelin Guide: the experts weigh in.	Think Zagat or Amazon: users review and vote on everything.
Advertiser/ Publisher role	Publisher establishes channel and controls content to gather an audience for the advertisers who sponsor channels or programs.	Build relationships by sponsoring (not controlling) content and interaction when, where, and how customers want it.
Strategy	Top-down strategy imposed by senior management drives tactics.	Bottom-up strategy builds on winning ideas culled from constant testing and customer input.
Hierarchy	Information is organized into channels, folders, and categories to suit advertisers.	Information is available on demand by keyword, to suit users.
Payment	Cost per Thousand (CPM): Emphasis on cost; Advertisers buy with the idea that share of voice = Share of mind = Share of market.	Return on Investment (ROI): Invest in marketing for future growth and profitability based on measurable return.

What makes the social web so important is that it permits companies to have these kinds of dialogues more efficiently and less expensively than ever in the past. Google is a good example of a living brand that fosters dialogue. Its features, in fact, actually enable dialogue between users—features like Google Talk, Google Groups, and Blogger. The brand has become iconic because it's an indispensable part of everyday life for anyone who uses a computer. Google is always developing new features, asking for feedback on "beta" elements, and checking to see what people do with Google.

In the new marketing, companies gauge brand equity not by static measures such as brand recall but by dynamic measures such as customer word-of-mouth. One useful tool is the net promoter score (NPS). A metric developed by loyalty guru Fred Reichheld, the NPS indicates how likely your customers are to recommend your company to friends or colleagues.

To see NPS in action, consider GE Healthcare's experience. The company recently asked 20,000 customers worldwide about the likelihood that they would recommend one of GE Healthcare's businesses. When the NPS score for its European diagnostic imaging business came in low, the company dove deeper and learned that customers wanted GE to respond more quickly to technical problems. By redesigning the response system, the company reduced the average response time from 40 minutes to just 10 minutes.

Not surprisingly, the NPS went up as response time dropped. And GE Healthcare's brand equity clearly benefited, with a direct connection to the bottom line. "GE has thousands of internal metrics on financial and operational performance," says Peter McCabe, GE Healthcare's chief quality officer, "but the only way I'm ultimately going to grow my business is to have customers tell others about us and buy more from us."[1]

Segment by What People Do, Feel, Think

As I said in Chapter 1, companies have traditionally segmented their markets according to easily identifiable demographics like age or gender. In the second period of marketing, they added lifestyle factors such as diet or medical concerns. With the advent of the social web, the new marketing means segmenting by what people do and feel— their behavior as well as their attitudes and interests. Your goal is to identify groups of customers within the larger market that you can reach and affect through your marketing.

Segmenting by behavior, attitudes, and interests doesn't depend on faceless numbers (how old customers are or how wealthy they are, for instance). Instead, it groups people by what's important to them, as indicated by what they do, think, like, and dislike. Once you know what moves your customers, you can target them with marketing activities that are meaningful to them. (It's all about them, after all.)

Targeting by Behavior

The old way of targeting was by demographics. This has probably been beaten into marketers' heads because it tends to be the way to buy media. Not in the new marketing. Now the Web helps us map behavior (on the Web itself) very closely. Age, sex, educational level, income, and other demographic indicators do not even register online (with the exception of websites for children or for products like liquor, where age is very important for legal reasons). As the famous *New Yorker* cartoon pointed out, on the Web, nobody knows if you're a dog. Software can track behavior, however, through the sites customers have been visiting, how long they linger on each page, and many other details. This opens the door to precise targeting opportunities.

Suppose a customer begins visiting websites related to flat panel television sets. One place she might look is on CNET.com. If you are Samsung, you might buy a link on CNET that says, "Special today on Samsung flat panel screens! Click here." The customer doesn't have to deal with the whole Samsung website but is taken right to a description of a very targeted offer.

Ultimately, the social web will lead to targeting customers who say, "Here are the things I like. Make me an offer, instead of my having to do all the work." Customers will be more open to targeting based on behavior because they've made the choice, they have the control. Marketing is not an irritation or an interruption if it relates to something customers want. The ideal is to get your brand in front of just the people who are interested in your product or service at this time.

This applies to paid media as well; paid media needs to support the growth of social media. For example, Samsung should also be sponsoring forums on what people like about its flat panel television sets or doing consumer comparisons with Panasonic or Sharp sets. It should participate in blogs that talk about flat panel television sets.

One of the big changes happening with the social web is a swing away from one-to-one targeting. I think marketers went too far in that direction, to a point of diminishing returns. We don't need to know every little thing about an individual. We do need to know that an individual participates in three or four online communities of interest on any given day. We might learn, for example, that a customer is interested in a car today because he's visiting a community subgroup about convertibles. Targeting is moving more to groups of interests and behaviors rather than to a narrow one-to-one approach.

Communicate Interactively

The new marketing creates the platform of true interactivity. Add more dimensions to the communication, rather than having most of the communication flowing from the organization. So you might add the ability to search and query, which is similar to search; add dialogue; add comments; add personal reviews of products, services, experiences.

Communication is less about creating contained and controlled messages (as in the old marketing) and more about creating compelling environments to which people are attracted. Remember, the marketer's primary job is to be the aggregator of customers and potential customers. The marketer's secondary job now and in the future is to create compelling environments that attract people.

How do you create an environment that is a shared, powerful experience? Starbucks is a great example of environmental marketing because it is a physical place that people want to visit and stay a long time. Amazon is a great example of early environmental marketing because people actually hung out at the Amazon website. They wrote about the books they liked and didn't like and made lists for other visitors. Oracle and IBM are two business-to-business examples of how to create digital environments that are thoughtful, attractive, and foster interactive communication.

Content Created by Customers

In the new marketing, the best websites will combine professional and user-generated content (contributed by customers and potential customers). You're asking for this—encouraging it—when you create an environment where it's easy to talk about your products or services. Even when you pay for and develop professional content, user-generated content continues the dialogue.

Here's what I mean about balancing professional and customer-generated content. You have every right as, say, a leading energy company to post your thoughts about the future of electricity. Customers will let you know whether they agree or disagree. You can offer podcasts from an expert on energy from the University of California, who talks about the future of renewable energy. Again, customers will react to this professional content with their own content.

Another difference between the old and new marketing is that content is increasingly visual. You see it now with YouTube; you also see it on business-to-business sites like Red Hat, Cisco, and Motorola, which have visual content customers can watch, download, interact with, or all three. It's almost embarrassingly easy to create a video with a video camera, digital camera, cell phone, or computer. Of course, the video may not be very slick, but that is often the point.

Let me point out, at the risk of sounding profound in a clichéd way, that everybody has become media. So as you get into the social web, you are media. Individuals are media, organizations are media. They are writers, editors, and publishers, sorting, prioritizing, and presenting compelling content in an interesting way makes it important.

I had lunch recently with veteran CBS TV reporter, Morton Dean (who has since retired), and former CBS News director, Ed Fouhy. They told me that for many years the huge expense of broadcast journalism was the filming and editing. Today, however, the quality of visuals made on a shoestring is quite amazing. Small to midsize companies with a video camera and a computer can produce acceptable-quality videos to post on a website or e-mail to interested customers.

For example, a local dry cleaner can hand a camera to an assistant and produce a show called, "Here's how we take care of the spots on your dresses. We don't use harsh chemicals. We are environmentally friendly." The chef at an Italian restaurant can produce a show called, "How we put together today's special from my grandmother's recipe." Or, even more basic, "Going to the market with Chef Umberto," following the chef as he picks out tomatoes or cuts of meat. Be sure to allow questions for interactivity. "Gee, Chef Umberto, my zucchini soufflé didn't turn out. What did I do wrong?"

Viva Virality

Viral marketing is interesting because it is word-of-mouth over which you have no control. Before I go on, a word about silly virals such as the "Subservient Chicken." At www.subservientchicken.com, a camera reveals a person in a chicken costume standing in a dingy living room. The chicken responds to typed commands, such as "tap dance," "take a bow," or "do push-ups." In the 17 months after it appeared, the site was visited more than 422 million times.

The site won a Grand Clio in the Internet ad category for Crispin Porter & Bogusky in Miami. Although the site barely mentioned Burger King and I've never seen anything to indicate what it did for the company, the Subservient Chicken's popularity prompted the entire advertising industry to look for viral ads that were funny, charming, sexy, or controversial, then e-mail them to friends or post them on websites.[2] My 10-year-old son, who is interested in Google video now, thought it was a howl when he found an animated hippopotamus singing a song, and he kept e-mailing it to his friends. So even at a 10-year-old's level, we can see the effect of virality.

Yet silly virality, for all its popularity, is not really word-of-mouth. The concept we should be talking about is content-based virality. How do companies get solid viral content, something that does more than simply attract attention to itself? In healthcare, the content could be about lowering cholesterol or improving quality of life. People talking to other people about these topics will create a viral dialogue with content.

Also, because of the stupid Subservient Chicken, marketers have created this expectation for virality of millions—422 million hits. I think virality can work in a far more controlled and smaller community-based way than having to reach a hundred million people to be "a successful viral campaign." In any event, marketers should always be thinking about powerful content that people will want to share and make it really easy to share.

A whole new generation of technology companies is working on this very issue. There's ExpoTV, sort of a cross between YouTube and *Consumer Reports*. ExpoTV makes it easy for anyone with a video camera to share ideas, information, and opinions about everything from arts and crafts to video games and players. This field is evolving, but the point is: Be sure your site passes the share test. Stop thinking about the Subservient Chicken and think about more engaging content that will interest smaller groups of customers.

Five Stars for Reviews

In the old marketing, customers turned to professional book, theater, movie, and restaurant reviewers for knowledgeable opinions. Once Zagat and Amazon invited ordinary people to give their opinions, there was no stopping the trend, the "Zagatization" of everything. *Consumer Reports* and the experts will always have their place, but in the new marketing, expect customers to vote on everything from cruise lines to cookware.

Customer reviews become particularly important for things that people don't do very often—such as rafting down the Grand Canyon or buying an ultralight airplane. Reviews include big ticket items, drugs, cosmetics, and many other things that affect the body. They will also be important for local and small businesses to enhance the experience of being part of a family of customers. If you add local search—the ability to find an Indian restaurant in San Diego or a bed-and-breakfast in Ashville—the reviews become exceptionally powerful. You may keep your ad in the Yellow Pages, but why not spend a little time, effort, and money to build your social media site?

In short, don't try to control your customers. The difficulty in the movement toward the social web is the natural instinct of marketers and corporate culture to control the message and the customer. It's difficult to give up control completely, but realize that reviews, as user-generated content, serve to demonstrate your company's transparency.

Advertiser and Publisher Roles: No Paper Needed

We have fewer reasons to kill trees because advertising and publishing for the social web requires no physical objects. Many of us simply throw away the instruction manuals that accompany our products, anyway. In fact, let's put all manuals on the Web. If I threw the manual away when I bought my microwave four years ago, invite me to download another copy from the website or click to watch a brief video.

The new marketing will be collateral free, with material that is more compelling, customized, visual, and up-to-date. Information can be a powerful customer relationship tool, but it doesn't have to be printed in an ad or booklet. Not long ago, while talking with a senior Home Depot executive, I suggested the retailer offer downloadable videos showing customers (and prospects) how to install a deck, build a shed, replace a light switch, winterize a home.

Ideally, you want to make content available at the exact moment customers need it. Let people choose what they want to see and when they want to see it, in effect making customers copublishers. The same holds true for advertising. Give up control, give customers real choices (and real content), and their collaboration will make the dialogue more meaningful. You can sponsor a site or community and associate your brand with it, but don't expect to control the dialogue.

Strategy from the Bottom Up

Strategy has traditionally been imposed from the top down. Now it has to be bottom up. As marketers, we have to learn from the people who are really paying attention to our products. Companies should test ideas and products and let the strategy bubble up from there, instead of trickling down from top management. Through the social web you can quickly test, say, 2,000 versions of a new yogurt container and build on the winning version. Suppose you develop a new diet pill. Where should it be displayed in chain drugstores? Where would a prospective customer look for this kind of product? Test that and use the results to drive your strategy.

Clearly, there are other dimensions to strategy. Market leaders must have an overall strategy to stay on top in the automotive industry, soft-drink industry, computer industry. But in a social web world, you have to segment your strategies to the various communities in which you want to participate and sell. If you're an automotive company, how do you communicate to the group that is interested in environment and energy conservation or the group that cares about speed and sexy looking cars?

Note that the principles here are the same for companies of all sizes, both consumer and business-to-business. Say you manufacture and market shopping carts. How do you communicate with supermarkets, chain drugstores, and other potential customers? Some will be interested in durability, some in looks, some in price. How can you provoke a dialogue so that customers tell you about problems their stores are having with carts or what shoppers are saying about carts?

Hierarchy: Let Users Decide

In the old marketing, information was arranged into channels, folders, and categories to suit advertisers. In other words, the sponsors practically dictated the hierarchy of organization. Not any more. With the social web, information has to be available on demand by keyword, when and how users want it. So when I need to change the cartridge in my ink-jet printer, I have to be able to find that information quickly and easily. Similarly, Samsung should have its information link immediately available to prospects who enter an appropriate keyword ("flat-panel TV").

I'll talk more in later chapters about how information—words, pictures, and sound—on the Web is becoming more and more convenient. The point is that customers want what they want when they want it, and in a way that makes sense to them. This may not necessarily be the hierarchical organization that makes sense to the advertiser or its information technology department.

Companies have traditionally used cost per thousand (CPM) to gauge advertising costs. How much will it cost to reach one million people at prime time in the Boston metro area? How much will it cost for an ad in a magazine with a circulation of 600,000? Notice that CPM puts the focus on the cost that the company must pay.

The new marketing has an entirely different emphasis. Instead of thinking about cost, you'll be thinking about return on investment. Your marketing payment will be based on a measurable return. For example, you might pay according to customer lifetime value (how much a customer is likely to spend with your company during the "life" of your relationship with that customer). In a highly sophisticated situation, the calculation would include the value of that customer's word-of-mouth and referrals.

From this perspective, marketing to the social web is truly an investment in your brand's future growth and profitability. You're paying for that growth, but you have a better idea of what you'll get for your money because the technology allows for more precise monitoring and measurement.

In the new marketing, customers want to be in charge of their own payment options. Whether they use a credit card, give you a bank account number for debit, or choose PayPal, payment options must be fast and easy. From your end, payments via the Web are easy to track and help you analyze where the company's revenue is actually coming from—down to specific customers and offers. That's a big payoff.

Test Driving the Social Web

Now that you know the 12 ways that new marketing differs from old marketing, what can you do to take advantage of these changes? Let's try a thought experiment: What would Ford do if it were planning to market to the social web? What would I do if I were suddenly (and improbably) responsible for Ford's marketing?

First, I would want to understand what has worked and what hasn't worked in traditional marketing, so I would begin with an assessment of past efforts. I would then prepare a customer map, paying close attention to the communities I see as the natural Ford communities. These would include current and former Ford owners of every type of vehicle.

Next, I would prioritize Ford's vehicles from the biggest selling vehicle to the slowest seller, not only in absolute terms but in the rate of change from one quarter to the next. Where are sales growing, shrinking? Why have the best-selling vehicles been popular? What is the problem with the ones that don't sell?

I would look at the Ford dealers, their successes and their dissatisfactions, to see what has worked for them and what hasn't worked. What distinguishes the most effective dealerships from only average dealers? I would look at the manufacturing and how that is tied to product quality and success of the vehicles. And I would look at the unions—what's good for them, what's bad for them, what Ford can control, and what is out of its control.

As an outsider looking at the corporation, I would advise Alan R. Mulally, the new CEO who came from Boeing, that Ford has lost its dialogue with its community. Job number one in the new marketing is to rebuild the dialogue through trust, openness, quality, and all the values that reputable companies hold dear.

After this analysis, I would start to build digital Ford. I would ensure that the voices of all those communities were heard—and listened to—regularly and seriously. This means hearing what Ford could do better on the cars, what it should get rid of, what models drivers, dealers, and service technicians like or dislike—and why.

Not only would I set up consumer advisory panels, I would set up dealer advisory and service technician panels. Ford should know what policies and procedures the dealers like, what they don't like—and why. These online forums would be password protected and not open to the general public, but it would be a way that the dealers could communicate directly with company executives and with each other.

Since 9/11 people have been taking more car vacations, so I would start thinking about ways to shift the focus off any negatives about Ford. Although negatives must still be acknowledged and allowed on the Ford website, I would showcase the value Ford brings to different customers in the form of family vacations, travel tips, fuel efficiency, and saving the earth. These are all issues in which a Ford Motor Company should be involved—moral purpose issues that cut across the customer communities. I would look at energy development and costs; how the population boom will affect the environment when billions of people own (or want to own) cars; the future of the dealership and how Ford can help its dealers.

Part of marketing to the social web and encouraging a dialogue with customers is also about shaping a future together. In my view, Ford hasn't been shaping the future as much as it has been trying to catch up. In other words, it's been reacting rather than setting a standard like Toyota does—a standard that people admire.

All this would be Phase One of credibility building and community interest building and future shaping. In Phase Two, I would bring some fun back to the brand. Cars are about more than getting people from point A to point B. They've become digital centers, entertainment machines, as you know when you pass a minivan with a color video screen for every child in the back seat. For fun, I would look for some experiential things, perhaps a new and fresh twist on the old Ford Punt, Pass, and Kick Contest, which was popular in the 1960s and 1970s.

I would start focusing on the user experience. How can I make Ford into the Apple Computer of automobiles through elegant design and understanding how people actually use their cars? By focusing on the user experience, I would bring in community building, digital communication, partnerships with entertainment companies and content providers, loyalty and discount programs, and even games. I would limit traditional advertising and start experimenting with cutting-edge ideas. Ford could make more use of new media, hold a car design contest for high school students.

Bold Moves for Ford?

Interestingly, as I was writing these words, Ford announced it was discontinuing the Taurus model and launching Ford Bold Moves (fordboldmoves.com), a website designed "to present Ford as a company coming to its senses, open to new ideas, and ready to learn from its mistakes." The site features links to news stories about the management shift and pulls no punches. One headline announced that company losses reached $5.8 billion during the most recent third quarter.

Posted segments feature officials of major environmental groups denouncing Ford for building gas-swilling sports utility vehicles and pickup trucks. In one, Ford Executive Vice President Mark Fields tells an audience of coworkers, "I've mentioned to you many times that the clock is ticking. Well, I want to be very blunt with you. Time is up. Time is up. We have got to fix the business, and we've got to fix it now."

Ford Bold Moves also presents critical articles by freelance business journalists. One describes U.S. heavy equipment makers Deere & Co. and Caterpillar Inc. and asks why these two firms remain world leaders while American car companies have lost their way. On the positive side, the site hosts a series of short documentary videos that offer behind-the-scenes views of the company. One shows Ford's "Warriors in Pink" competing in car races to raise money to fight breast cancer. Another reports on a Ford dealer who's opened a service station selling 85 percent ethanol fuel for use in Ford "flex-fuel" cars, which can run on ethanol or gasoline.

Site visitors can post responses to the videos and articles and ask questions that the company will answer. One question I saw asked: "Why do you produce a car and then discount the price? Why not produce a car that is worth the sticker price?"

Here's the problem with Ford Bold Moves. Because Ford and its advertising agency do not seem to trust their customers, I see the website as more Madison Avenue manipulation. On the first look, the site appears really earthy and down home. Clicking through, all the videos are beautiful, showing beautiful Ford vehicles near the ocean or crossing a famous bridge. The videos are almost purely Ford commercials.

Then there's the text. Ford says, in effect, "This is here to open our world to you. We want your help. We will post anything that comes— negative or positive. We have made some mistakes, and there are some passing negatives and gee, we have made some financial errors." At the bottom of the first part of the website a disclaimer says, "Any content and/or opinions expressed in this website, including without limitation, message boards, articles and responses to questions are solely the opinions and responsibility of the person or entity named as the author and do not necessarily reflect the opinions of the Ford Motor Company. You also understand and acknowledge that you are responsible for the content of any message that you post to this site."

After reading the disclaimer, I posted a few comments that were not terribly negative. They never appeared. So I decided to make up a horrendous story and watch for a reaction. Silence. The whole thing is manipulative and insults the intelligence of the customers who visit the site.

Seth Godin, author of several books on Internet marketing, thinks Ford is wasting its time. "Ford doesn't have a PR problem. Ford has a we-were-dependent-on-gas-guzzling-SUVs-until-people-learned-the-truth problem. Ford has a we-don't-reward-great-designers problem. Ford has a dealer problem." Godin says that unless the company gets its cars right, no amount of Internet marketing will help.[3] I say that Ford has to do both, and that an effective dialogue with *all* its customer communities can help it get its cars right. But fordboldmoves.com is not the way to do it.

I can understand the reluctance of Ford's management to open itself up to the slings and arrows of outrageous fortune, so in the next chapter I'll talk about some of the real problems of the social web.

CHAPTER 4

How to Let Customers Say What They Really Think

(And Keep Your Job)

Should you let customers say whatever they want on your website? You (and, truth be told, your boss) might instinctively recoil from this idea. And that's understandable, considering all the negative comments floating around the Internet.

Just a five-minute search will show you the depth and breadth of customer dissatisfaction with American business practices. Here, for example, is what Thomas (no location listed) wrote on complaints.com: "I e-mailed Ford Motor Credit about getting some sort of incentive on buying another new truck with us spending about $45,000 for the vehicle.

I asked if they would give me any incentive considering I was a Ford client for at least 25 yrs. They responded back by thanking me for my loyalty and giving me a rebate that was equal to my previous truck payment. That was $750.00. I was fit to be tied. I realized they don't give a rats a whether I am a previous client or not. I went to Toyota and bought my new truck. I never realized how incredibly well built the truck was and how well it ran. I then proceeded to sell my wife's Excursion and we bought her a new Sequoia. That is a beautiful well built SUV. I will never buy from Ford again and I expect them to belly up like GM because they lost what was important. They produce low quality vehicles and they don't take care of the customer. Toyota will surpass them soon enough and they deserve it because of the quality product and service they continuously provide."[1] This, I suspect, is exactly the kind of comment Ford does not want showing up on fordboldmoves.com.

Michelle (no last name given) from Texas writing to Wal-Mart on the my3cents.com site (and here I'm quoting, typos and all): "I was hungry and I ate a chocolate bar off of your shelf, it was only 68 cents so I did not think that it would make a big difference to a store that makes billions a year. As I was leaving the store I was stopped by security and arrested for shoplifting, over a small chocolate bar. You guys make millions a year and you get uptight when someone takes a chocolate bar from your stores. I am banned from your stores for a year, well I do not care, if you are going to get stingy over a chocolate bar then I will not want to come back anyway. I am going to the press to tell about how stingy and selfish you are. For f*cks sake it was just one chocolate bar."[2]

I could go on and on, but you get the idea. So back to that thorny question: Should you let people post their comments (the good, the bad, the ugly) on *your* website?

Learning to Let Go

When I suggest that companies allow ordinary people to comment on—even criticize—their products, services, or store security policies as part of marketing to the social web, the reaction is something like: "Gee, I don't know if we can do that. What am I going to tell my boss?"

The simple answer is: Tell your boss that people are going to criticize anyway, and you're probably better off in the long run letting them do it in your store (or on your site) than in the public square.

The question actually has a number of parts. What are the disadvantages and advantages of allowing public comments on your site? What are the legal issues—libel, plagiarism, defamation? How can the organization be both open and protect itself?

In this first phase of the social web, I believe websites, microsites, webinars, and communities should be a combination of professional content and customer-generated content. But as a first tentative step into this ocean, you might limit the site to only those tools over which you have total control—podcasts and the sites themselves. You don't have to open your site up to anyone; you can have the professional content developed by experts within your company. All companies— Wal-Mart, Vonage, Ford, IBM, Hewlett Packard, even small businesses—have various subject-matter experts on staff. Let your experts express their opinions and thoughts on the site, which they can do without giving away the store. What they say is content your organization can control.

You can also offer content from selected experts. For example, HP has John Gallant, the editor of NetworkWorld, host a regular Q&A podcast series that HP's customers and potential customers can download. Although this is content over which your company has less than total control, presumably the outsiders will not attack their hosts any more than a freelance newspaper columnist will attack the paper.

To ease into customer-generated content, I suggest that companies set up at least one place as a forum where customers and anyone who is interested can talk about your products and your company. Start with one product—maybe a product that's a great product you can make better. Don't put out your worst dogs first to be kicked around. In the beginning, at least, you can try to direct the conversation toward your strengths. Then, as you slowly develop trust over time— both with customers/prospects and with senior management—you can open the site to other, more sensitive, topics.

Most of the comment software you might use to screen public comment allows you to choose which comments you want to leave out. In the simplest form, such software acts like a spam filter (you probably know how this works because you have one on your computer). But in addition, there are programs that flag obscene or sensitive words: "sucks," "rip-off," "incompetent," "low quality," and whatever words are touchy in your situation. Someone will have to actually read the flagged posts and decide which should be posted.

Inevitably, every organization will receive negative comments. They will range from "Wal-Mart banned me for a year for taking a 68-cent candy bar" to "My grandmother was killed when her Pinto was rear-ended." Fortunately, just because you invite public comment, you do not have to publicize every comment. John Palfrey, who is the director of the Berkman Center for Internet & Society at Harvard Law School, recommends a relatively flexible policy on posting. "If something is unrelated or is spam or both, you delete it," he tells me. "And if somebody says something critical of your product, I think you need to be able and willing to rebut the criticism. Take it head-on."

One of the lessons learned in protecting or promoting a brand online, John says, is that it rarely makes sense to ignore your critics, adding, "By virtue of offering a space to comment on your company, you are inviting those critics right up to your front door. You have to be prepared for them whether you're letting them on your site or you're just reacting to what somebody else blogs elsewhere."

Critical information about a company and its products has a way of slipping out anyway. For example, *Automotive News* reported that Mazda dealers Randy Hiley and Robert DeVaux made what they thought was a routine video webcast after the Mazda National Dealer Advisory Council meetings. In it, they mentioned that customer complaints about the RX-8 sports car—squeaky brakes and engine flooding—were unfairly lowering customer-satisfaction scores. Hiley and DeVaux told dealers: "Mazda is well aware of the negative impact on the scores caused by the RX-8 surveys. They agreed with us that the situation had to be changed. And so, effective July 1st, RX-8 will continue to be included in the survey, but the scores will no longer be included in the results."

Someone copied the video and posted it on a Mazda RX-8 enthusiast website (rx8club.com). From there, the story spread to autoblog.com, an auto enthusiast site. Some unhappy RX-8 owners took the dealers' private webcast comments as evidence that Mazda and the dealers were unwilling to repair their cars swiftly and thoroughly. Autoblog.com noted: "Why would RX-8 owners be surveyed if those survey results were not a factor for the dealer in the end? And more importantly, what incentive would dealers have to give RX-8 owners good customer service if these surveys weren't being counted?"

Here's what Mazda spokesman Jeremy Barnes wrote to members of the Mazda RX-8 forum: "That video is only one portion of the story behind our survey. Mazda's goal is to ensure that our dealers provide all customers, regardless of the vehicle they own, with the highest level of service and customer satisfaction. To assume, after viewing a video posted on the Internet, that Mazda would do anything to compromise this is simply and unequivocally wrong."

Now the carmaker and its dealer council are looking at new ways to communicate with dealers. Said Hiley: "With technology the way it is, it doesn't matter if it's video or e-mail correspondence. Obviously, somebody can get that information somehow. What it tells you is we have to find another medium to communicate with our dealer body that has some security to it."

Ironically, after the webcast circulated, J.D. Power and Associates issued customer-satisfaction scores showing that the RX-8 was Mazda's highest-scoring model. "Those people love their cars," said Robert DeVaux. "The few dealers who sort of put this on the table may have been overreacting."[3]

Comments as Early Warning Signs

I don't know whether Mazda aggressively addressed the issue of squeaky brakes and engine flooding in the RX-8—it sounds as if the company was more concerned about the security breach and satisfaction ratings than the car's shortcomings—but management should have used this dustup as an early warning of possible trouble ahead. Consider the experience of Dell.

When Dell refused to fix or replace his broken computer, Jeff Jarvis, the creator of *Entertainment Weekly*, began posting "Dell Hell" comments on his blog, BuzzMachine. When he had no reaction after several days, he posted an open letter to Dell Chairman Michael Dell and Chief Marketing Officer Michael George, in which he outlined his struggles with customer service. It struck a nerve with the public. While BuzzMachine frequently receives more than 5,000 visitors per day, Jarvis's "open letter" became the third most linked-to post on the blogosphere one day after it was posted. Traffic on BuzzMachine skyrocketed to more than 10,000 visitors a day (according to Intelliseek's BlogPulse) as other people commented about their bad experiences with Dell customer service.[4]

"What is the NPV [net present value] of Jeff Jarvis' complaint?" asked Pete Blackshaw, the chief marketing officer of Nielsen BuzzMetrics, on his blog. As cofounder of the 2004 Word-of-Mouth Marketing Association, Pete has more than casual interest in this subject. "It's not only the lifetime revenue or 'buyer power' he brings to Dell (probably $15K of buying Dell products over a 15–20 year period), but more importantly, the 'viral power' of his referral network or circle of influence (easily over $200K . . . probably way more)," he wrote.

Call centers and consumer relations departments tend to look at consumers in a vacuum, said Pete; they don't consider customers' circles of influence. "Rarely will you find a website feedback form that asks consumers whether they blog, spend time on message boards, or share their recommendations with others. Ad agencies and CMOs wax poetic about the importance of profiling, but this thinking rarely seeps over into 'consumer affairs.' We need to reframe our mindset to think about all customer interactions, especially feedback, as an 'advertising' opportunity. If Jeff Jarvis is satisfied with a product, and bothers to speak out, we should have models to estimate the incremental consumer-generated media (CGM) he might generate on behalf of the brand. If he's pissed or frustrated or deeply dissatisfied, our CRM systems should be able to predict with reasonable levels of confidence how much trouble or negative CGM he might stir up. Moreover, this should be a calculus we apply to all consumers, not just the big fish like Jarvis. That said, no one can say Jarvis didn't catalyze a critically important conversation."[5]

There's more. The Jarvis/Dell cause célèbre was high-profile enough that it sparked a white paper, "Measuring the influence of bloggers on corporate reputation," by Market Sentinel (an online monitoring service), Onalytica (a U.K. stakeholder analysis firm), and Immediate Future Ltd (a U.K. public relations agency).[6] The paper concluded, "Jeff Jarvis's BuzzMachine is the key online source for those who have a negative perception of Dell's customer service; its influence is enhanced by support from a closely allied group of bloggers; Dell's own influence on the topic of its poor customer service is weak; Jeff Jarvis's BuzzMachine is the key source for low-influence stakeholders (normally bloggers) writing about Dell customer services in general; taken all in all Jeff Jarvis's BuzzMachine is the eleventh most influential voice on Dell's customer services in general; if the bloggers were aggregated they would be the second most powerful influence on perceptions of Dell's customer services after Dell itself."

In Dell's defense, I suspect there were a couple issues involved here. First, it's sometimes difficult to isolate the truly important complaints from all the "noise." It's akin to the situation you face every working day: Which of all the problems demanding my attention today must be addressed before they become crises? Second, if a particular product happens to have an exceptionally high number of defects, this may overwhelm a system designed for fewer faults. Nevertheless, the Web means that anyone with a grievance can publish it so all the world can read about it (and I mean this literally).

If you don't start having a dialogue with customers on your site, they will attack your company anyway. As the bloggers become more and more influential (and as it becomes easier and easier for a casual visitor to find relevant blogs through better search tools), a company that has not engaged its customers in dialogue will be at a disadvantage. It would be like ignoring reporters' calls from the *New York Times* or the *Wall Street Journal*. In fact, ignoring negative comments is the equivalent of "No comment," which is the biggest communications mistake executives make. The advantages that come from having openness—which leads to trust, confidence, and respect—outweigh the disadvantages—which lead to suspicion, fear, and contempt.

I'm amazed at how many companies are unaware of the conversations about them already happening on the social web. Senior executives are often shocked that people are talking about everything from safety to design in automobiles, and from efficacy to side effects in drugs. These are deep and broad conversations yet much of the corporate world doesn't know they exist.

Try this: Type "complaints" and the name of your company into a Web browser, and see what's being said about you and your products. While the complaint sites seem to accept almost anything and some of the complaints (like the ones I quoted at the beginning of this chapter) are off the wall, you may find issues to investigate further. Soon the complaint sites are going to be like traditional media; there are going to be wacky ones, but some will rise to the top and become as influential as *Consumer Reports*.

Trust is another major reason to allow critical comments on your site. Andrea, a twenty-something urbanite, tells me she has bought several items from Overstock.com. The site, like Amazon, Netflix, Circuit City, and others, allows customer comment and although Andrea has posted some mildly unfavorable remarks, they never appeared. She suspects Overstock.com is screening comments and not posting the disapproving ones. As a result, she says, "I don't trust *any* of the comments on the site." Trust once lost is almost impossible to regain.

On the other hand, Amazon.com has permitted critical reviews on its site since 1997, although it offers guidelines and says it will not post reviews that do not follow the rules, which are things like "focus on the book's content," "don't reveal crucial plot elements . . . profanity, obscenities, or spiteful remarks . . . phone numbers, mail addresses, URLs . . ." and the like. Nevertheless, within Amazon.com there are some scathing reviews: "The quality of this book is truly subpar. There are virtually no areas of the book that stand out. It is a poorly structured, hashed-together book with little insight. There is a lot of fluff."

What about Legal Issues?

Having your dirty laundry aired in public is one thing, but exposing the company to legal liability is an even bigger worry. Senior executives should consider the legal issues involved in opening a site to public comment, issues such as libel, defamation, and plagiarism. It's natural to worry that the company may be exposed to a lawsuit because of what a customer posts on the website. For example, what if an anonymous writer claims on your site that one of your dealers stole a customer's down payment? What if a writer claims to have found a severed finger in a bowl of your company's chili?

I'm not going to spend a lot of time on the law here, for two reasons: (1) I'm not a lawyer; and (2) even if I were, these are issues for a lawyer who knows your state's laws. For a good all-purpose introduction to the law in this area, check out the Electronic Frontier Foundation's "Legal Guide for Bloggers" (www.eff.org/bloggers/lg/) and its comparable legal guide to podcasting (http://wiki.creativecommons .org/Welcome_To_The_Podcasting_Legal_Guide).

That said, in general, a libel is any statement that falsely charges any person with crime, or says falsely that someone has been indicted, convicted, or punished for crime; imputes in someone the presence of an infectious, contagious, or loathsome disease; imputes impotence or a want of chastity; or "tends directly to injure someone in respect to his office, profession, trade or business, either by imputing general disqualification in those respects that the office or other occupation peculiarly requires, or by imputing something with reference to his office, profession, trade, or business that has a natural tendency to lessen its profits." Trade libel is defamation against a company or business's goods or services. (The finger in the chili is a trade libel.)[7]

Obviously, if the company libels someone in response to a complaint, that's a problem. But what if a customer, writing on your site, libels someone else—a dealer, a salesperson, a competitor—or plagiarizes copyrighted material? Again, I'm no lawyer, but I think you'll probably be protected under Section 230 of Title 47 of the U.S. Code, which was passed as part of the Communication Decency Act of 1996. Section 230 says, "No provider or user of an interactive computer service shall be treated as the publisher or speaker of any information provided by another information content provider," as federal law, it preempts any state laws to the contrary.

In practical terms, the Electronic Frontier Foundation says that customer comments, "entries written by guest bloggers, tips sent by email, and information provided to you through an RSS feed would all likely be considered information provided by another content provider. This would mean that you would not be held liable for defamatory statements contained in it." The foundation also points to evolving case law: "However, if you selected the third-party information yourself, no court has ruled whether this information would be considered 'provided' to you. One court has limited Section 230 immunity to situations in which the originator 'furnished it to the provider or user under circumstances in which a reasonable person . . . would conclude that the information was provided for publication on the Internet.'"

John Palfrey tells me that while the legal situation is not 100 percent clear, "it is relatively clear that those who host an online service have a safe harbor under Section 230 that indemnifies for most things—people who provide space for other people to post something. My guess is that most companies would be able to avail themselves as a safe harbor site. I don't think it's a big concern."

To sum up, I understand your boss's reluctance to let customers say what they really think on your site. At the same time, I'm convinced that the benefits outweigh the dangers. You don't have to allow anybody to say anything, any more than you have to accept every spam message that shows up in your mailbox. Still, you're better off allowing your honest critics to have their say because it gives you an opportunity to either explain why they are mistaken or to correct what they've discovered.

You might as well allow customer comments because people are going to criticize you anyway, as Dell, McDonald's, Genzyme, Amway, Starbucks, and other companies have found. As John notes, "There is a sliding scale between constructive feedback and aggressive, destructive behavior. Absolutely, there are people whose online comments will be highly negative, aggressive, and destructive to a company's brands. It's a very real and very difficult problem." In my view, this should not prevent you from soliciting *constructive* feedback.

I have no problem with the nice videos on fordboldmoves.com. However, the company needs to be clear that the site is like the special advertising sections in magazines and newspapers, the so-called advertorials. Freelance journalists often write the copy, but it is still a special advertising section, because companies are paying to be included in the coverage. When such material is clearly labeled, I have no problem with it.

I do have a problem with material that is digitally trying to masquerade as real editorial, real social media, real transparentiness (which has the same relationship to transparency that truth has to truthiness). It's fine to have slick, professionally produced video . . . as long as people know it is open, honest, and transparent. My favorite comment in a *Forbes* article about the site was that the advertising people are calling what they have done "brand journalism."[8]

If there are journalists who buy that, I would be astonished. If that's the evolution of marketing, count me out. Let me be clear: I respect paid media. Paid media in the new marketing world of the social web will have to have a huge role and is still working itself out with banners, buttons, click-throughs, video, brought-to-you bys, downloaded pages, live commercials for live events, and more.

If I were running Ford's marketing, I would take a different tack. Rather than a digital advertorial (or infomercial) called fordboldmoves, I would create a site called makingFordbetter and invite public comments and discussions in as transparent a way as the First Amendment permits. I'd actually show how customer comments were incorporated into Ford's vehicles. Yes, I'd have less control, but I'd be sparking more conversations and—I hope—building more trust.

Seven Steps to Build Your Own Customer Community

CHAPTER

5

Step One: Observe and Create a Customer Map

(Otherwise, You Can't Get There from Here)

Marketing to the social web is increasingly important, but is it right for you and your customers? To avoid the "build it and they will come" syndrome, you have to do your homework, build a solid foundation for your community, and get a dialogue going. So Part II of this book is all about the seven steps and four platforms you need to harness the power of marketing to the social web.

First I'm going to outline the seven steps and then explore each step in more detail, chapter by chapter. To show you how the process works, I'll use Saturn as an example. Assume, Saturn has four large competitors fighting for the top spot among its particular target consumers: Toyota, Hyundai, BMW Mini Cooper, and Honda. The competitors have been gaining ground and consumers no longer value Saturn as a

groundbreaking leader in automotive manufacturing and business practices. Management wants to reestablish Saturn's position as the leader
of this industry.

If Saturn were a client (it is not) and if Saturn management
wanted to market to the social web (and I have no idea what Saturn's
management is up to these days), we would first observe what is happening on the Web as it relates to Saturn. That takes us into step 1.

Steps to Marketing on the Social Web

1. *Observe.* Go into the social media and the blogosphere to understand the most influential places within the social web. What
   are the largest communities? What are they talking about? What
   is the relevant content? For Saturn, we would search throughout
   the blogosphere to track conversations from bloggers, analysts,
   automotive writers, and consumers. What are they saying about
   the company, its products, and its key competitors? Which automotive brands are generating more buzz and which are the focus
   of the conversations in the digital world?

2. *Recruit.* To shape a community, you must enlist a core group of
   people who want to talk about your company, your products,
   things you are doing, where you are going. This second step is
   based on the research collected in the first step—you have to
   know who your recruitment efforts should target.

3. *Evaluate platforms.* What are the best platforms for your marketing goals? Blogs? Reputation aggregators? An e-community?
   A social network? (Each of these is worth its own chapter.)
   Some combination of these, or all four? What kind of search
   tools? Is your audience more interested in listening to things
   than reading? Are they interested in seeing a lot of things? Do
   they want to have questions and answers all the time? Do they
   want to edit?

4. *Engage.* Engagement is all about content. How do you build relevant content that will get people coming, talking, responding? How do you build the mix of professional user-generated
   and enterprise-generated content to do that? Here's where you
   really get the dialogue going.

5. *Measure.* This is self-explanatory, although more difficult to do that it might seem at first glance. What do you need to measure? What is your community really connecting with? What are the most relevant metrics?

6. *Promote.* While some sites do not need much promotion (think MySpace or YouTube), most do. You have to get out to the other communities. You have to use the social media to get people talking so they will come back and download things. You have to advertise just as if nothing had changed.

7. *Improve.* Make it better. Add improvements to the site; make it more convenient, more useful, more friendly, more rewarding.

Now back to our Saturn example. In the "observe" step, after searching Saturn's name, the names of its cars, and its services (e.g., the cars can come installed with the GM OnStar system), we would search for key influencers in the vertical automotive websites, those that specialize in news and information about cars. One way to find these influences is based on keyword searches. Another is to use search tools, such as Technorati, Google Blog Search, and others, to narrow the focus. Saturn might suggest keywords such as "automotive services," "top automotive marketing," and "peace-of-mind driving."

Assume that after we researched the blogosphere and the Web, we learn that Saturn is not taking advantage of the music subsection of the automotive websites. Suppose we find that Saturn's competitors are leveraging the music industry to promote their automotive products and services through free music downloads, iPod connections in their vehicles, and concert sponsorships. Assume further that Saturn heavily endorses the music industry, but is not mentioned as often as its competitors in conversations on the Web.

The insights we take from this observation step show that Saturn is not dominating the digital channels. Other automotive companies are generating more buzz from their online campaigns. We learned that the drivers in Saturn's target market were embracing online tools that make it easier for prospective customers to find information. Also, even though Saturn has been a tremendous supporter of the music industry, it is not promoted at large music industry and festival sites. With these insights, Saturn's management now has a direction and a goal to begin planning the next steps.

With this as a quick overview, let's dig deeper into how you can take the first step and observe.

Look Who's Talking

During the observation phase, you want to find out what—if any-thing—people are saying about you on the Web. Are you being talked about in these new channels and platforms in the digital world? Are any blogs covering you? Are any blogs saying anything about your cars? (If you're General Motors, they are. In fact, they're talking about your cars even if you are as obscure as Stanguillini Motors.)

Observation helps you get a handle on the landscape. You'll dis-cover what is being said and the conversations that are going on about your company, your products, your category, your competitors, your enthusiasts, your detractors, your suppliers, your partners. These are the groups most important to the fabric of your business.

Who's talking is as important as what they're saying. You need to figure out who is more influential in what is being said. Although 9,000 blogs may have mentioned your car, there may be only 10 that are critical to your reputation, that are growing, and that are becom-ing as authoritative as *Motor Trend* or the *New York Times.*

All of this applies not only to large corporations, but also to fairly small or medium-size companies. Remember, the digital world is a big place with a lot going on. You're likely to find conversations that dis-cuss what you make, what you do, who you compete with, what your customers are saying and buying. No matter what your size, there are digital conversations about you, your industry, and where it is going. (If there actually are no conversations, you have an invaluable oppor-tunity to start one.)

In addition, you have to analyze the influence of new media. This is similar to the media kit that newspapers and magazines have always produced. For instance, check how each medium matches the demo-graphics of your audience: how much money your customers make, where they live, what they eat.

You Need a Business Goal

Within this first step of marketing to the social web, there are a number of research guides that a company should establish before proceeding:

- Identify and prioritize the company's needs and goals.
- Important dates that will determine when in-market activities will need to start.
- Target audience definitions—whom are we most interested in getting a point of view from?
- Products/services to be searched.
- Which languages to search.
- Top four or five competitors.
- Best practice comparisons. Which competitors within the industry or in other industries are using the digital channels to their advantage, particularly social media?
- Keywords for searching the Web.
- Tools audit. Which tools (if any) are we already using to monitor, track, and report?

It should be obvious—but it is not always—that before you begin to think about marketing to the social web, you must have a business goal or marketing goal of some kind. Is there a target market you want to reach more effectively? Do you want to reach a certain market more often? Do you want to change the message for a particular market? You might set a marketing goal around an event such as a product launch. Or you might be experiencing—or think you are about to experience—a crisis of some kind: a product recall, a government investigation, a strike.

Start by defining the business goal you are trying to achieve through this whole activity and come up with important dates. For instance, if the business goal is a successful product launch of a new product, nail down the date that product is launching and whether there is any kind of prelaunch beta period or anything that might affect the launch.

Define the Target Audience and Speak Their Language

Then you need to define the target audience. Whose point of view is most important to your business? What customer group is your most immediate focus? Do you care about teenagers? Do you care about Java developers? People with diabetes? Quilters? Big 10 football fans? You can define the target audience by behavior, demographics, topical interests, or whatever is relevant to the business goal.

This is an absolutely critical point. As in other marketing efforts, the more precisely you can define your target audience, the more effective your marketing will be. You may discover, for example, that the behavior you are looking for is among people who don't use the Internet much. I have assumed up to this point that the target audience you are trying to listen to and later influence is in fact on the Internet. That may not be true, and once you learn your target is not on the Web, you may want to review your business goals.

You also need to define which products or services are relevant to the business goals. With a new refrigerator, as an example, are you going to look at energy efficiency, recycling issues, service experience, dealer comments, cleaning tips, or some other aspect? With a new sandwich shop, are you going to consider nutrition (a must), variety, breads, condiments, beverages, music, in-store ambience, take-out service, environmental impact? What do people care about? And if you find an issue that the target market seems indifferent toward—such as environmental impact—should you care anyway and take it into account?

You have to decide what languages you are going to search. While English is on its way to becoming the universal language, if you're a global company doing business in France, Germany, Spain, Japan, China, or any country where the Internet is significant and English is not, you need to search in the native language. The Japanese are the most active bloggers in the world right now. You should figure out what languages are relevant and have someone with the appropriate skills conduct observation.

Look for Best Practice Examples

Given your business goal and target market, you want to look at competitive websites (or the subdomains of the websites) with an eye toward identifying best practices in managing digital conversations. Carefully examine the features and functions and the uses of social media on your competitors' websites and relevant subdomains. Ideally, you should select one or two websites outside of your direct competitive set that can serve as best-practice examples of specific elements.

For example, Oracle did a flash piece called, "Who Caught John Blade?" (I found it on the Oracle.com site and it may still be available if you search.) This piece was probably made from a high-end video that was originally produced for major account sales calls. Essentially, it's a who-done-it mystery that takes viewers through a case example of a close call with a terrorist bomber trying to get into a nuclear power facility with a vanload of dynamite. The movie follows characters from the local Georgia police department, Homeland Security, and the Savannah River Nuclear Power facility as they work on their computers, send information back and forth, and try to connect the dots, starting with the theft of dynamite from a construction site all the way to the arrest of the alleged terrorist.

At the end of each snippet of the story, an Oracle spokesperson explains the different Oracle tools used by the characters to swiftly narrow down what is going on and eventually catch John Blade before anything happens. After Oracle made the piece and released it, there was a relatively big splash but that was the last I heard about it. Still, when I first saw it, I thought it was an awesome use of social media. "John Blade" is very interactive, it tells a story, which is always a great way to capture attention in marketing activities, and it is a cool story. It's an excellent example of communicating compelling product information in the digital world.

Another example of how to use social media is IKEA's site (Ikea.com). Click the "Ask Anna" button to bring up an avatar, a graphic representation of an IKEA customer representative that is animated by computer technology. Her text message says, "Welcome to IKEA. I'm Anna, IKEA United States's Automated Online Assistant.

You can ask me about IKEA and our products and our services. How can I help you today?" If you type, "I want to redo my bedroom," Anna takes you immediately to the "Beds and Bedding" pages of the site. Given the number of items for sale on the IKEA site, this is an utterly painless and simple way to search for what you want.

Avatars are fairly common now, and studies have found that using an avatar sales agent leads to more satisfaction with the retailer, a more positive attitude toward the product, and greater purchase intention. It is another cut on search functionality and another way to avoid calling the retailer and going through 47 menus in the automated phone system. In principle, the avatar gets customers to their destination faster than clicking or calling and it may help reduce customer calls, which reduces the retailer's costs.

Select Key Words and Begin to Search

Next you want to select 10 to 15 key words, the search terms that lead you to the blogs, the news sites, and the communities that are discussing, mentioning, or rating the topics that concern you most.

Now you're ready to embark on your search. You can use a number of tools here. "Snorkeling tools" (like Cymphony, BuzzMetrics, Nielsen's Brand Pulse, Intelliseek, or Metrocity) can identify where you're being mentioned. Search tools (like EveryZing) can help you check for mentions in video, podcasts, and audio files.

But before you begin, find out if somebody within your company is already auditing online conversations. Quite often when we go into a company and propose we do this work, we find that somebody is already using a snorkeling or search tool. Does somebody in your corporate communications, your interactive group, or your Web group (or whatever it's called in your company) have or license any proprietary tools? If so, use them.

All the Internet tools exist for searching have their strengths and drawbacks. The Web is a Wild West in terms of these tools. But there's a counterintuitive aspect to this: You might assume that because something is on the Web, you'll be able to find and measure it in a very detailed way. Unfortunately, that's not quite true. You have to understand what and how the tool is measuring. And you have to understand and relate what the tool measures to what you're trying to discover.

For example, a free tool called Alexa can search URLs. Type a URL into the Alexa search function and it will tell you the traffic ranking by week, by month, average page views, and more for the way Alexa measures traffic. Here's the catch: Unless the material you are searching incorporates the Alexa tag into its own code, Alexa doesn't pick it up. So the Alexa ranking is only meaningful within the Alexa sphere.

But even if your company has licensed a proprietary tool like Cymphony, you should probably start with what we call the "reputation aggregators," any search capability-type site where the results are automatically ranked: Google, Yahoo, MSN.

Now comes the grunt work for which there is no shortcut, no silver bullet. You must search one site after another, using the parameters you have defined and working hard to stick to them (because it is embarrassingly easy to get sucked down rabbit holes). This absolutely requires a pair of intelligent eyeballs connected to the brain of someone who begins to learn the players in the blogs, in the communities, and on the news sites. This person also has to get to know the issues and the lingo at least as thoroughly as somebody who works in the domain. In time, someone with this ability begins to recognize the rhythm of the conversations that are going on and can identify the hot topics and the trends.

This part of the process is difficult to describe exactly. There is no replacement for simply doing it. Use several different Web searching and tracking tools, an extensive database of key influencers and the conversations they have about the product and service, then look for patterns in the key words generated. If you have well-defined parameters, in three to five weeks of reading blogs, forums, postings, and community sites, you should have your finger on the pulse of what is going on.

For example, assume your business goal is a new product introduction. How do you connect your observation to this goal? Think about your best prospects for this new product: What are the characteristics of those prospects? What are the types of things they will want to know? What will interest them in your product?

Now look around the Web to locate where those types of people tend to hang out. What blogs do they read (or would they read if they existed)? What communities do they belong to, if any? The answer could be "none," but if your product is new software, for example, you are going to find all kinds of communities. While you are reading through all blogs, news sites, and communities, in the back of your mind you should ask yourself: How can we influence the folks on the Web who influence our prospects and customers? What you find in this observation step may surprise you.

Take consumer travel, for example. Say you market vacation packages. Based on your business's situation, your parameters might include a target audience of people 55-and-older who have traveled outside the continental United States at least once in the past two years; English language sites; and three or four key potential destinations—Hong Kong, Shanghai, Kyoto, and Seoul. You might find (to your surprise and delight) that the thing people talk about most is currency conversion—how to do it, how to think about it. Currency conversion turns out to be a very hot topic. Conversations pop up about whether to bring traveler's checks, an ATM card, a credit card, a debit card, or convert money before leaving home. People want to know how much hard currency they should carry and what is the best place to find information on the exchange rates.

Now you've got an interesting insight. You started off wanting to know how best to reach consumers who are interested in planning to travel to the four destinations that you have chosen. Currency conversion turns out to be a major topic of interest. If your particular customers are talking about it, your company should become "the" source of information on the topic. Build a community of people who know about, have had experiences with, and can make suggestions about currency conversion. (I'll talk about these steps in the chapters ahead.)

Create a Customer Map

So far I've referred to a target market in terms of the prospective customers a company wants to reach to sell its products or services. But that, of course, is much too narrow a focus. A company of any size targets many customer groups interested in the organization (some authorities call these "stakeholders" or "constituents.")

In this first step of observing the Web, you should identify who is saying what and which customer group they represent. A case in point is Saturn, which I used as an example early in this chapter. Saturn should be able to identify at least 10 customer groups: the people who buy the cars, the dealers who sell the cars, the service technicians who repair the cars, the finance people who finance the cars, the workers who build the cars, the regulators who rule on emissions and safety, insurance companies, parts suppliers, independent service shops, automotive writers, and more.

While these are all specific and definable groups, they may overlap to some extent. An employee may also be a customer; a dealer may also handle the financing. Nevertheless, it is important to identify all these different customer groups and understand their wants, needs, and concerns, to create a customer map.

This is a key point. Customer communities are not limited to the folks who buy from you. Indeed, given your particular situation, your employees may be a more significant customer community to which you should be marketing. The community of your dealers may be able to offer each other more tips, ideas, and solutions than your own dealer relations people. It is important, therefore, that senior management map all these customer communities to ensure that no group is overlooked and that the groups are periodically ranked.

To sum up, the first step in understanding the social web for the marketer is observation. Don't stop at snorkeling. I often hear comments like, "Oh gee, my brand appeared in this blog or that blog. I Googled the company and I have this list of everything." That is snorkeling from the surface.

What I call observation involves diving deep into the social media and the blogosphere and understanding the most influential places within the social web world. You might find that Boing Boing is very powerful with a *New York Times*-type reader and has more influence on the East Coast than in the Midwest and that it talks about these five topics. Or you might find that iVillage is important to teenagers and young women. Or that theknot.com is rapidly becoming the most important site for prospective brides. Or that yelp.com is reviewing restaurants, nightlife, shopping, and more in New York, Chicago, San Francisco, Boston, and more.

Here's an example. You're a pharmaceutical company selling diabetes drugs and want to know the fastest growing, most important sites or blogs related to diabetes and diabetics. Which ones have the largest communities? What are the members talking about? What is the relevant content on a daily basis? How about the professional e-content of places like MedPundit.com and WebMD.com? Much like the *New England Journal of Medicine*, there are digital versions of professional content.

You observe the blogosphere, the community sites, the forums, and other places where people are communicating with each other on the Web, and start looking for threads, topics, places where people are commenting. You are definitely going to observe news events, the more traditional things that organizations have watched for years. But now you look for what is getting picked up and the chatter about it.

Once you have done the observation step ("done" rather than "finished" because in a sense, it is never finished because the world continues to move), it's time to begin recruiting community members.

CHAPTER 6

Step Two: Recruit Community Members

(With a New Toolbox and Your Own Marketing Skills)

oes this sound familiar? "We tried a podcast . . . a microsite . . . a webinar, but nobody came. It was a waste of time and money." It's a complaint I often hear when I talk to executives about marketing to the social web.

Even when you observe what people are saying online about your brand and company, even when you map the various communities you want to attract, you can't just create an online presence and put out a sign saying: "Here we are." The "build it and they will come" strategy might have worked in the Internet 1.0 world of 1994, when websites were still novelties (and unfortunately, some companies haven't abandoned this outdated strategy). But those days are gone forever.

Maybe it's a human impulse to believe that what's mine is better than what's yours, and companies fall into that trap just as individuals do. They believe that if they make a website exciting, lively, colorful, and feature-rich, it will be better than other sites and attract attention. Your site may, in fact, be better, but so what? What's in it for the customer? The customer needs a real reason to show up. And that's where recruitment comes in.

Recruit as if Your Business Depends on It

Recruiting for the social web is serious business. Why? Because once people have been recruited to one or more communities, they tend to become impervious to traditional media. In fact, according to compete.com, an online research firm, over one-third of the people who participate in online communities spend less time watching television and reading newspapers or magazines as a result of their increased usage of social networks. (That makes sense. A day still has only 24 hours, and the more time customers spend on the Web, the less time they have for other media.)

The impact of diminishing audiences is magnified by the increasing influence online communities have on the products their members buy. Nearly 75 percent of the people who spend time online say their colleagues are the primary influence on their purchase decisions, and 63 percent consider reviews and product comparisons from other consumers to be as credible as expert reviews from independent third parties.

This trend of using the social web to inform buying decisions and circumventing marketing messages is sure to continue and spread. More than one-third of consumers said in a recent study that in the future they will rely on product reviews found through forums and online networks more frequently. Already, 20 percent of consumers surveyed reported that, based on information they found online, they purchased a different product than the one they originally intended to buy.[1]

If you don't recruit people, if you don't engage them with meaningful content, you'll get run over by the speeding locomotive the social web has become. Only by recruiting members and getting your site ready for the online community can you put the power of the social web to work for your business goals.

Bring a New Toolkit to the Job

At the start of this chapter, I mentioned an all-too-common lament: a company opened its site and nobody came. Let me suggest two reasons why people might not come to your online party. First, there was little or no outreach to the social web; and second, the content was not compelling enough. You need a definite plan for attracting and retaining community members. And that's where your marketing knowledge and skills come in.

Marketing to the social web does *not* mean forgetting everything you've learned. It does mean using a new toolkit or approach to build on what you already know. You'll need new and different perspectives on how you connect with and relate to consumers, but the basics of good strategic and tactical marketing communications don't change. You're trying to generate leads, produce revenue, and exert influence; you're trying to generate brand awareness, induce trial, and build customer loyalty. It's the old lather, rinse, and repeat from Marketing 101.

None of this is particularly revolutionary, but it's absolutely critical. You already have some idea of how to address many of the questions raised by marketing to the social web. Now it's time to put your skills to work by recruiting members for your online community.

You recruit online community members the same way you do in the offline world, but it is much easier and richer online. A good starting place is to think about the reasons why people join online communities at all. According to Compete Inc.,[2] there are four reasons:

1. *Meet people.* Some 78 percent of the people who visit online communities join them to communicate with others, either colleagues or new acquaintances with whom they develop relationships.

2. *Entertain themselves.* Another 47 percent join to find entertaining content such as photos, music, or videos.

3. *Learn something new.* Some 38 percent join because they want to obtain information about topics that hold particular interest to them.

4. *Influence others.* And 23 percent join to express the opinions in a forum where their ideas can be discussed, debated, or acted on.

Note: These add up to more than 100 percent because some people participate for two or more reasons.

Send Out Your Invitations

With these four reasons in mind, you can start crafting an approach to recruiting members to your community. Perhaps the simplest and most direct place to begin is with the names and addresses available in company databases. These may come from warranty cards, contest entries, dealer lists—any source your firm has used in the past to build a mailing list.

Another simple recruiting technique is to print the site's URL on product labels and invite people to join. You should certainly include the URL in all your printed company marketing materials—catalogs, brochures, direct mail, and advertisements.

You can buy a list from a research panel company much the way you would buy a list for a direct mail effort from a list broker. These are opt-in lists of people who have chosen to receive e-mail communications (which distinguishes this approach from spam). Send those people an invitation to join your community. Your e-mail invitation has to be as engaging and attractive as any direct mail piece. Be sure that when people respond, they find themselves taken to a website where they would like to be. Otherwise, with a click, you'll be added to the spam filter.

More broadly, recruiting to the social web consists of two toolkits: digital media marketing and digital media relations. Digital media marketing creates branded community-based destinations and invites people to come to them through the sources I've just mentioned and through paid advertising. These destinations could be webisodes (cartoons or a short film—often in installments—used to promote offline events or products), microsites (a website developed with a particular focus for a specific target audience), a contest, or a viral experience. Digital media marketing can cover the spectrum from kooky viral videos to very serious targeted microsites that might be targeted at a very narrow (or not so narrow) target audience that you want to reach with your product or service.

As an example, the site 43things.com has found an interesting way to build communities. The site invites visitors to list things they would like to do with their lives: Improve my vocabulary . . . practice yoga . . . backpack through Europe . . . have a secret underground lair . . . the list is endless. "It's more like a life list than a to-do list," says John Peterson, one of the site's seven founders. "It's not about the 10 things I want to do this week; it's more about the 10 most important things in my life that I never write on my to-do list."

What makes the site interesting is that when you create your list, you are automatically connected to everyone else within the 43 Things universe who want to accomplish those same goals. At that point, you can write to those people and they can write to you; you can share ideas, setbacks, and successes. In other words, just by expressing your goal, you join the community.

Think of digital media relations as next-generation public relations. It has the same goal as traditional public relations—to engage in and influence conversation in a prescribed channel. In the digital world, these are online spheres of influence, which include reputation aggregators, blogs, e-communities, and social networks. The approach you use with digital media relations is somewhat different from the approach used in traditional public relations, because the digital channel is, to some extent, disintermediated by the online spheres of influence.

In offline public relations, firms have to work through the traditional print and broadcast channels. They have to get to know the right writers, reporters, and editors, the right analysts. They have to know the people who influence or decide what newspapers and magazines publish and what radio and television stations broadcast. Online the process is similar, but a bit more open. However, that is becoming less and less true as the online spheres of influence gain in influence.

For example, six months or a year ago, you probably could have written an e-mail to the CEO of, say, Tech Crunch—a weblog dedicated to profiling and reviewing new Internet products and companies—and if your message was at all newsworthy, it would have been posted the next day. (Remember that most reporters and editors are always looking for good, new information.) Now, given the site's growth, a message like yours might not appear today, tomorrow—or ever.

If digital media relations means influencing opinions, attitudes, or behaviors, how you go about it depends on the channel, the goals, the product or service, and the company life cycle. What is your marketing goal? How you recruit community members depends on the business objective for starting the community, both the near-term and long-term business objectives.

Create That Community Feeling

I asked Tom Gerace, the founder and CEO of Gather.com, about companies starting online communities. Gather.com is a community where engaged, informed adults can connect over everything from food to politics to travel to gardening to health to money to movies and much more. Members can express opinions, ask questions, post pictures, rate articles, and form subgroups.

Should marketers expect that if they build an online community, people will show up and participate? Tom says, "I think in most cases they won't. It's not just the technology. The social networking platform is a critical component, of course, but equally important is the community and the quality of the experience that members of the community create for other members. So, when marketers think about launching social networks, they need to ask: Why would people want to form a community around this place, this brand, or whatever it happens to be? There are very few brands that people feel such an affinity for that they want to link their personal identity to the brand in a persistent way. And few people feel connected to other human beings because of their mutual affinity to a particular brand."

Of course there always exceptions. Harley Davidson comes to mind as a brand/product around which owners will gather. Another example: Lego Group, which promotes the Lego Ambassadors as a community-based program in which adult Lego hobbyists share their construction, product, and event knowledge with the worldwide Lego community. They are not employees, but "contribute to the Lego fan community without the promise, expectation, or receipt of compensation. The Lego Ambassadors Program is an officially recognized community-based program of the Lego Group."[3]

But does someone who uses, say, a Macintosh computer want to socialize with other Mac owners—online or offline—just because they all own Apple products? Probably not. They're unlikely to go out of their way to find other Mac owners unless they're true geeks, the 2 or 3 percent of owners who absolutely love Apple and its products.

Jeep encourages community feeling by trying to get owners to wave to other Jeep owners. "I am actually a Jeep owner myself," says Tom, "and I love going off-road. But do I want to meet other Jeep owners? No, I want to be with my four friends in the Jeep."

Gather.com suggests that, rather than trying to climb the very steep hill of convincing consumers to form some social relationship around the brand identity itself, agencies and advertisers participate in existing social spaces. "Marketers need to get their minds around the idea that the social space is inherently different from traditional media," Tom explains. He points out that in the social space, content comes from trusted, known sources. This confirms your own experience: You know whom you believe for anything from a movie recommendation to book recommendations to introductions to other people to job references. So in a social space, the content is almost guaranteed to be relevant and to be trusted if you believe the people are trustworthy (or you don't listen to them).

"Because you have exceptionally high degrees of relevance and trust," says Tom, "other people trust the content you place in the social networks as a result. The question is: Do you feel the same level of affinity or trust or love for a brand that you do for another individual? I think the answer is no. Can a brand build that level of affinity? Probably not. Brands don't give love."

In his view, what is driving the social web and why people spend so much time on these sites—a point that many marketers haven't yet grasped—is that people benefit from exploring the lives of friends, family, colleagues, and strangers with similar interests and concerns. The explosive growth of social media such as MySpace reflects that benefit; they have a huge reach right now and their reach is still growing. As a result, Tom advises that companies get involved not by building a community around the brand but by "going into established, successful communities and creating value, which will tend to attract more people to the community."

Diane Hessan, the founder and CEO of Communispace Corp., brings up another key issue to consider when recruiting members: "In general, it's harder to recruit people for a community involving a low-involvement product or service than for a high-involvement product." Communispace develops collaborative online communities for company clients—more than 225 at this writing—as a way to connect marketers and customers and provoke insights that companies can use.

In Diane's experience, the issue of involvement affects recruiting for all kinds of products and brands. "If a client said to us, 'We need people who fly on airlines a lot and who want to be in an airline community,' it would be a lot easier to establish that community than, say, a toilet paper community," she says. "As it turns out, a lot of companies in the toilet paper business want to build communities and understand their customers, so we finally figured out a number of things that must be done to recruit people to these communities. It's not rocket science, but you have to be thoughtful. Sometimes companies lose perspective and they think, 'Oh, wow, what we do is so important and so interesting, people will want to be part of our community.'"

Diane also points out that even when people register at your site, they may not actually continue in the community: "Sometimes people will sign up, go in, decide it's really boring, and not participate any further. In the meantime, the company is saying, 'We have one million visitors!'"

To sum up, you're facing a two-part challenge: recruiting people to the site in the first place and keeping them engaged once you get them there. I'll be talking about the second part in the next chapter.

Build on Existing Sites and Communities

Instead of trying to form an entirely new community around your brand—which is clearly very tough to do—you might start a community to add appeal to a website you already have. Let's say you're in the travel business and you've set up a microsite for enthusiasts interested in traveling to sporting events around the world—World Cup Soccer, Olympic Games, the Roller Marathon International in Dijon. Your microsite would also appeal to somebody interested in going to the World Figure Skating Championships in Gothenburg, Sweden. How could you build community around this microsite?

First, link your site to the event's official website as well as to other figure skating sites such as frogsonice.com, isu.org, and figure-skating.com. A part of the online experience for this target segment is going to be community where people can share content about destinations, content that can be text, photos, and video. Your links will help people find and exchange this kind of information. They'll also serve to recruit members in an indirect way.

Next, locate experts in figure skating and in travel to Sweden. Look for folks who have something material and interesting to say. Maybe they're knowledgeable about the sport and the skaters, or they've closely followed winners of previous skating championships. Find people who have special—and up-to-date—information about places to stay and eat in and around Gothenburg, Sweden. Your experts should be able to offer advice about getting around the country, interesting side-trips, and so on.

It helps to put yourself in the shoes of someone who's interested in the content of your microsite. If you cared enough about the World Figure Skating Championships or the sport of figure skating, you probably would visit the site every few days or once a week to see what's new. Maybe someone has posted an interesting comment or quote; maybe another member has reacted to something you posted. And if you spotted special travel offers or other offers on the site, you might check those every now and then. You might return if you found occasional interviews with athletes or coaches—even with the athletes' families.

Now think about the microsite as a whole, not just the skating enthusiasts. Recruit 10 or 20 experts in each of the several geographies where upcoming international-level sporting events will be held. They'll be community members but clearly identified as experts. You *must* be transparent so that if your experts have a relationship with an event, a hotel, a restaurant, or anything else they discuss, this must be very clear to site visitors.

You'll want to have compelling content for seeding until the site gets enough momentum to meet your business objective. The level of that momentum will differ depending on your business purpose. This is why you'll need a marketing plan, a course of action, for obtaining content and building momentum to attract and engage your customers and prospects.

Feel the Momentum

One good way to get momentum going is by seeding your community with quality content that inspires people to talk up the information and the site to others. In any community, you're going to have participants and lurkers—folks who visit the site but never ask a question or post a comment. The lurkers are important, too. A lurker may take an action that is important for the overall objectives at some point—she may book a tour for example—and lurkers may tell friends about the site, encouraging those people to visit and participate actively.

Other ways to recruit are the good old-fashioned ways. Remember the principle of don't forget what you already know. You want to look at the business case for online advertising, offline advertising, traditional public relations, online public relations or digital media relations, paid search, and more. Getting people to come to your community and then return again and again means you must have something they care about enough to come back for. It's as simple and as hard as that.

What other sites do you need to go to for recruiting purposes? What kind of paid media should be used? Perhaps you should buy ads on Google to bring people to your community. As I've said before, the Web allows you to measure your advertising's effectiveness and you can see the most important places your customers come from and go to.

Planning for recruitment requires a mindset. Ask yourself: Which are the most powerful media? Where are my customers going? Where are my competitors? Here's an analogy: When advertisers created a 30-second commercial, the agency had to think about the lighting and the music, the movement, the message, and the logo. For a website, you do the same kind of thing. You're developing an environment that will present information, allow for interactivity, draw like-minded people, and create transactions. You're not creating marketing material, you're creating a digital environment.

Does direct marketing online have a role in marketing to the social web? Does public relations online have a role? Does paid advertising have a role online? Yes, yes, and yes. But the goal of all those tactical, executable things is to create a theater of sales, to bring people to rich, thoughtful, interesting online communities.

And once you've brought them to your community, what can you do to keep them coming back?

CHAPTER

7

Step Three: Evaluate Online Conduit Strategies

(And Don't Forget Search)

Who do you want to reach? What do you want to say to them? Those are the key questions to think about as you plan your conduit strategies—your plan for using the social web to reach your target audiences. The big four conduit strategies are reputation aggregators, blogs, e-communities, and social networks.

And don't forget search, for the simple reason that you want people to find *you*. Search comes in two flavors: unpaid—or organic—and paid, which can offer a nice return. Wyndham Hotels & Resorts calculates that for every $1 it spends on search advertising, the firm generates $14 in revenue. Small wonder that Wyndham has increased its spending on search advertising by 500 percent since 2001. Roughly two-thirds of its online ad budget—and close to 15 percent of its total marketing budget—goes to search ads keyed to phrases like "Bahamas hotel" and "Phoenix golf." Kevin Rupert, Wyndham's vice president of marketing and strategy, says: "Search marketing is a basic foundation—you have to have it."[1] I couldn't agree more.

This Way to the Conduit

Before I explain the big four in more detail, I want to emphasize that the lines of demarcation between reputation aggregators, blogs, e-communities, and social networks are somewhat permeable. The line between e-community and social network can blur, meaning it's hard to say where an e-community ends and a social network begins. The line between blog and reputation aggregator is definitely blurry: Important blogs and the links they cite are very important, and so the blogs themselves are reputation aggregators targeted at a relatively narrow audience. The bottom line: Conduit strategies are not black and white.

This chapter paints the big picture; in Part III, I'll detail how you can actually use each of the big four conduit strategies effectively. Now a bit more about them:

- A reputation aggregator is a site that provides rankings of content/sites. People use these sites to decide what content they want or need. Examples include Google, Yahoo, Ask, and MSN among others. Reputation aggregators are a key—perhaps the key—gateway for all users to reach online content.

- A blog (or weblogs, although only pedants call them that these days) is a digital diary; authors create dated journal entries (with or without images) that others can comment on. In the same vein, a vlog is a video blog.

- E-communities are online sites where people aggregate around a common interest area with topical interest and often it includes professional content. Examples include WebMD, iVillage, DailyCandy.

- Social networks are member-based communities that enable users to link to one another based on common interests and through invites. Examples include eHarmony, MySpace, Friendster, and more.

The *social web*, by the way, covers all four conduits, although you could argue that an e-community site that has no dialogue with its members is not really part of the social web. Also bear in mind that the conduits will continue to change, just as what was considered a website in 1993 would hardly be considered a website today.

Another point: Marketing, advertising, and public relations people often talk about "platforms." There are really two platforms: the actual physical or electronic platform—a newspaper ad, a television commercial, a magazine article—and the communications platform.

To be clear, this chapter is about the online conduits you can use to communicate your platform, not the electronic platforms themselves. The communications platform involves analyzing who you're trying to reach and what you're trying to say. So think about questions like: What do we stand for? What is our position in the marketplace? What are the messages we want to get out to our various customer communities? Is our audience more interested in listening to things than reading about them? Are they more visual, interested in seeing a lot of things? Do they want their questions answered? Do they want to comment about, say, a drug's side effects, a computer's performance, a politician's behavior?

Again, you don't need to forget everything you already know as a marketer. You're not starting from scratch when you market to the social web. You're just adding some new sensibilities and perspectives to your toolkit.

Searching, Searching

As you formulate conduit strategies, consider how search engines (which act as a form of reputation aggregator) rank sites. The rankings can vary widely based on a site's age, content, keywords, structure, and links to other sites. In addition, think about how prospects, customers, partners, financial analysts, and other people might go about finding your product or company online. Because some percentage of these people will find you using search engines, you can't ignore where your site comes up in the search results. The good news is that you can materially affect search results using unpaid media, such as blogs, e-communities, and social networks.

While search engine optimization has become an entire special discipline, the principles of organic search are fairly straightforward. Identify the hot topics and search terms that people are likely to use to find you. If prospective customers are not deeply familiar with your product or solution, they're not going to hunt for it. So try to imagine what they *will* hunt for and "tag" your site so it turns up. (A tag is a word or code assigned to items like Web pages or photos to facilitate searching and sharing. "Bahamas hotel" could be a tag.) If your site is not turning up on search results or is far down in the rankings, you have to start using the other three conduits as well as digital media marketing, otherwise known as paid search.

Your goal is to create branded community-based destinations to start the virtuous circle in motion: a person finds your site, comments, links to it, tells friends and acquaintances who tell their friends and acquaintances who link back to your site, and so it goes. And as the circle grows, your site moves higher and higher in the rankings.

More about Blogs

You hear a lot these days about blogs and the blogosphere (also blogsphere), a collective term encompassing all weblogs or blogs as a community or social network. Many blogs are densely interconnected; bloggers read others' blogs, link to them, reference them in their own writing, and post comments on each others' blogs. Since a blog is also a website, the term "site" and "blog" can sometimes be used interchangeably if a site has blog capabilities.

Is blogging right for your company or brand? Consider what role you want it to play. Do you want to play a thought leadership role? If so, blogging is probably a really good idea. Here's the big but: Blogging is a good conduit strategy only if you can imagine you or someone in the company becoming a publisher with an editorial calendar, an editorial agenda, and—guess what?—a writer.

The hard part is becoming a publisher with the responsibility for obtaining content, enforcing deadlines, and maintaining quality. This is very similar to Web 1.0 in the early 1990s when an executive might wake up one day and say, "I need a website and it has to go live in six weeks." And in 1993 or 1994—maybe 1995 for latecomers—the site might go up without the company figuring out how to keep the thing fed, fresh, new. The blogosphere is very similar—you have to be a publisher to make any impact at all.

If you can't commit to an editorial agenda and calendar, with an editorial strategy that supports your overall marketing goal, don't do it. If you're only going to post every six weeks, or every six months, don't bother. Don't wind up like the failures of Web 1.0, when people looked at a website, saw that it hadn't changed for weeks or months, and decided the company was either sleepy or clueless.

I'm still shocked when I visit a website, check out the company's press releases and links to news stories, and see that the most recent item is eight months old. Is the firm still in business? Are its managers so busy that they have no time to update the website? Has nothing newsworthy happened in eight months?

Don't set up an online newsroom if you can't maintain it; otherwise, the company looks moribund. Keeping a newsroom or company blog current requires an investment in time. Not only do you have the initial cost of setting up the mechanism, you have to consider the ongoing cost to maintain, whether internal time or an outside consultant's time and fee.

Nevertheless, as Jonathan Schwartz, the president and chief operating officer at Sun Microsystems, has said, "Leadership is all about communications, it's what leaders do. Almost by definition, your set of responsibilities comes down to who you pick to work for you, how much budget you give them, and then what do you say all day long when you are trying to motivate change and drive people forward. So blogging is a tool that, especially for leaders, is critical to amplify your communications."[2]

Welcome to the E-Community

E-communities offer professional content to members and allow member (or visitor) dialogue. In addition to the sites I mentioned earlier in the chapter, sites like IBM.com, Cisco.com, Sun.com, Microsoft.com, and behospitable.com (Hilton Hotels) are e-communities. No hard sell, but lots of interesting information and a chance to add ideas or ask questions.

Behospitable.com, for instance, has handy professional content like suggested toasts and ice-breakers. It also invites visitors to submit their own anecdotes about hospitality and tips for being hospitable. Of course, the site has links to Hilton Hotel brands and reservations as well as multimedia content about the company itself. It's up to the user to decide what to browse, what to contribute, and whether to investigate Hilton's offerings.

In the publishing industry, certain e-communities are starting to take the place of magazines. BusinessWeek.com is an e-community, as is Forbes.com, Smartmoney.com, Fastcompany.com, and many, many more. If the content is valuable enough, the site may even be able to charge a subscription fee (think *Wall Street Journal*).

Here's where your marketing smarts come into play. You need to clarify your marketing objectives and determine whether an e-community would help achieve these goals. If so, go ahead and create the site—with concrete plans for maintaining it. On the other hand, maybe you don't need a separate e-community. Depending on your situation and objectives, would you benefit more from participating in someone else's existing e-community? For example, the site money.cnn.com is the Internet home of *Fortune, Money, Business 2.0,* and *Fortune Small Business.*

Just as Welch's Grape Jelly might team up with Skippy Peanut Butter in a joint promotion, L.L.Bean with Subaru, so could a pharmaceutical company team up with Sermo.com ("a free online community by physicians for physicians") or a pet food company with Dogster.com or an airline with behospitable.com.

If you are a small company, you can search not just in these big-time online e-communities, but small trade groups—restaurants, opticians, liquor stores, specialty shops, all depending on your local market or trading area. But on e-communities, you are not only aware but can give opinions and answer questions.

Tap into Social Networks

Certain social networks—MySpace, FaceBook, Friendster—have received a huge amount of publicity, but there are actually hundreds more online. Nearly all require members to register, and some—like aSmallWorld, DeadJournal, and Doostang—require an invitation to join. You can market on a social network, but be very careful in the approach you take. In fact, before you jump in, study what other companies have done.

Reuters, for example, has assigned a technology reporter to cover stories within the Second Life virtual world. The reporter's avatar works out of a virtual home office in a virtual building that looks like a cross between Reuters' London and Reuters' Times Square buildings. Reuters has become the news supplier for Second Life, which at this writing has almost a million residents but is growing by double digits every year. Not only does Reuters enhance its brand by participating in Second Life, it also puts its reporter in a great position to pick up stories about Second Life—written just for Second Life members.

You probably can't release a movie today without having a presence on MySpace, among other social networks. What if you're marketing hardware or software, financial services or healthcare? Should you market on these venues? My advice is to be very prudent. Remember, "build it and they will come" does not apply online. "Blow it and they will slam you," however, definitely applies. Perhaps the biggest challenge of the online world is the speed with which news, ideas, opinions can catch on virally, both positive and negative. So choose your social networks with great care.

CHAPTER

8

Step Four: Engage Communities in Conversation

(To Generate Word of Mouse)

Up to this point, you've observed the field and created a customer map, recruited community members, and evaluated online conduit strategies. Now it's time to plan to engage your community (or communities) in conversation. Approach this as if you were writing a marketing plan with the target audience of customers and potential customers in mind. Your conduit strategies will guide many of the activities you plan. Of course a website (or more than one) will be part of your plan and of course it must have great content—"great," that is, *as defined by your target audience*.

95

How do you engage a community in conversation? Before I talk about the nuts and bolts, I want to show you a company that understands its target audience and has a variety of conversation-starters in its tool kit.

Bubbly Conversation

Jones Soda Co., based in Seattle, Washington, has been building a community conversation for years. First, a little background. If you haven't seen Jones Soda at your local Starbucks or Panera Bread, you may not know that the company differentiates itself by cooking up some very quirky flavors. For a limited time during the Thanksgiving holiday, for example, you can buy its Turkey and Gravy, Sweet Potato, Dinner Roll, Pea, and Antacid Flavored sodas. In December, you might sip its Egg Nog, Candy Cane, or Sugar Plum soda. Year-round flavors include Blue Bubblegum, Tangerine, and Crushed Melon soda.

Just looking at the soda is enough to start a conversation because the photos and sayings on each bottle have been submitted by customers (and sometimes by employees). But how do customers get into the conversation? Check the label, and you'll see the Jones URL (jonessoda.com). Now conversation is just a click away.

Jones involves customers in its brand and promotes a conversation in at least a dozen ways. Under the website's "community" tab are some very good examples. On the message board, for instance, "members" (visitors who log in) can post comments about Jones's products, its special events, and—gasp!—subjects that have nothing whatever to do with Jones. The guest book is exactly what it sounds like: a page where visitors can sign in and leave a quick note for Jones—a simple yet welcoming touch.

To backtrack to that label, customers who upload a photo or a saying through the website are more likely to visit regularly so they can find out whether their submission has been chosen. In fact, Jones encourages visitors to browse an ever-changing gallery of photos and sayings on the site itself. Although this may sound one-sided (customers submit and Jones picks), it actually generates dialogue because visitors get to vote on the best photo of the year.

The website has fun and games to bring visitors back again and again. Not long ago, it featured a Magnetic Words Page, where visitors could move words around to make their own sayings. But Jones also encourages customers to rate and review its individual flavors and to suggest interesting new flavors. These are good conversation-starters.

How about some direct customer feedback? "Survey Yourself and Pimp Your mySpace" is a link where Jones incorporates market research like this: "Are things looking a little dusty in your MySpace corner? Or how about just helping us with our new survey? We've got a bunch of nosey questions we need your help on and as a thank you we're giving away MySpace themes." When I last visited, the survey was asking about soft drink purchase habits, websites visited, and television shows watched regularly.

Here's my point: Jones does all this not just to sell soda pop but also to engage customers and potential customers in a dialogue.

A Brand Is a Dialogue

In the era of the social web, branding is the dialogue you have with your customers and potential customers. The stronger the dialogue, the stronger the brand; the weaker the dialogue, the weaker the brand. Thanks to the Internet, the dialogue can be active 24 hours a day, 365 days a year. It includes both the conversations you have with customers and the exchanges your customers have with one another—all related to the strength of the brand.

Apple Computer is terrifically strong in the social web by encouraging conversation around its brand. Apple dominates portable music with the iPod and its little brothers, the Nano and the Shuffle. Some of the iPod-like devices made by other companies are just as good if not better than the iPod, yet Apple owns 76 percent of that market because it keeps the dialogue going with its customers. Do you want the user experience to be faster? Do you want the machine smaller?

Do you want a better screen? Do you want to watch television shows? Movies? This kind of dialogue contributes to Apple's amazing brand power. It's not the only communication Apple has with its community: the company also uses traditional marketing and advertising to bring people into the online conversation.

Apple is good at building dialogue around product enhancement and user-experience, which in turn strengthens its brand. Another way to stimulate conversation is to use a moral purpose—renewable energy, fair prices for coffee growers, children's health, automotive safety, and the like—as the starting point.

Stonyfield Farm, for example, is deeply concerned about environmental issues. Known for organic and natural food products like yogurt, smoothies, and soy milk, Stonyfield mentions its pet causes on product labels and is always posting new content on its website (stonyfield.com). It has something to say about global warming, healthy eating, sustainable agriculture, supporting family farms, and much more. And it wants to hear what customers think.

The site's "Ask Our Nutritionist" page answers questions submitted by the community. The Baby Babble blog not only presents content about the trials and tribulations of parenting young kids, it asks parents to join the dialogue by sharing their ideas. The Bovine Bugle blog, about farm life from the cows' point of view, also generates its share of interesting comments from the community. People who gravitate toward the Stonyfield community for its causes can get involved by reading site content, voting on which nonprofits should receive Stonyfield's donations, and following links to various advocacy organizations. All this for a mass-market consumer packaged good.

Controversy is an opportunity to engage even more people in conversation. Stonyfield's home page recently featured a letter from the CEO, responding to a *BusinessWeek* article on the growth of organic foods. "The story generated a surprising amount of Internet activity which included some gross misconceptions and falsehoods about our company and our practices," wrote CEO Gary Hirshberg. He spelled out Stonyfield's position, bullet by bullet, asked community members to share their views by clicking to make contact. Even though Groupe Danone has a majority stake in Stonyfield, the brand has a distinct, independent identity because it keeps the conversation going on so many levels.

Let me make another point here: Company executives should stop thinking that they can buy a brand name or build a great brand simply by making big media buys. Neither Stonyfield nor Jones is buying a lot of media space or time, yet each brand has a sizable community of loyal followers. True, most managers in senior positions today grew up with the Super Bowl mentality—buy enough advertising and you create the brand. Those days are gone; I don't think any company can buy its way into a brand name anymore. The increasing importance of social media and social marketing on the Web is, I believe, tipping the balance and will have much more impact than media buys.

One more key point about making conversation in a community: Don't talk about what Merck stands for, or what Coke stands for, or what any brand stands for. You have to show this (like Stonyfield) and get a dialogue going. What does your company care about—from a social nature, from a moral nature, from an ethical nature? That is the high-level part of a branding dialogue. Then you have to do the everyday work of carrying on a dialogue about specific issues surrounding the products and services you offer. Stonyfield did this with its CEO's letter and its open invitation for the community to share ideas about the issues discussed in the letter.

To be sure, advertising has a definite place as a conversation starter. Genmar Industries recently used online, cable television, and print ads to get people talking about its Triumph boats. Genmar's agency, Republik, suggested differentiating Triumph on the basis of its toughness. Agency personnel hitched the boat to a pickup truck (no trailer), dragged it along country roads, slammed it into trees, and finally sent it skidding at high speed into the water. Yet, as you can see on the video at toughboats.com, the boat survived in style—tough, indeed.

Why post this "bubba test" video online and seed it on boat-related blogs and sites? "We can start a conversation with the consumer," Triumph's president says, "and it's measurable." Not only that, but it got media coverage in the *New York Times* and elsewhere, extending the audience and earning word of mouse all over the place.[1]

Making Customers Part of the Brand

Customers have always played a small role in the world of the brand, as research subjects, as enthusiasts, and as gadflies. Today, however, because of the Internet, you have to think of customers as transmitters of your brand conversation. They're already having conversations with one another about your products anyway, conversations about your cars or your music or your drug's side effects. It's up to you to ensure that your organization participates in that conversation and to convince community members that you care about what they think and say about the brand, the products, the services.

What customers and potential customers talk about is deeply connected to your reputation and your position as a brand in the social media world. That's why you have to part of the dialogue, no matter what brand you market. If you market flat screen television sets—although the product or service could be virtually anything—how do you contribute to the dialogue about, say, advancements in flat panel technology? One way you might participate is by explaining what makes a good flat panel screen, on your website and in other online forums.

You need to add your voice to the conversation in places where you can participate in transparent fashion, so it's clear who you are and who you represent. At the same time, you should link back and invite people to your site for more dialogue or an opportunity for visitors to just listen, for instance, to a podcast about the quality elements in flat panel screens (or whatever is meaningful to your audience). You might offer videos of your product in use or in development, allow the community to see the results of product testing, or have your service people post tips and answer questions. The more your customers are involved in the dialogue, the more they get involved in the brand.

Because a branded dialogue should be multidimensional, think about building a conversation around what you stand for, based on your activities. British Petroleum's Beyond Petroleum campaign was more than just advertising, as an example. It was a discussion about renewable energy, a great first step to set British Petroleum apart from other big oil companies. Similarly, Pfizer has stimulated dialogues about different diseases, with the implied message that "we are trying to make a higher quality of life for you; this is what we're about—not just making money." Remove the subject of transactions and profit from the brand dialogue and you actually add another dimension to the dialogue.

The dialogue, after all, changes to fit the community's interest. Does the ordinary customer care if General Motors makes money? Some may, but most care about a new vehicle. Does General Motors offer some good trucks at good prices? Do people like them? Are they reliable? Are they strong? Most prospective customers don't care what the stock is worth. A portfolio manager at UBS or Fidelity cares, and they care about a different brand dialogue or brand conversation.

The future of the Web is going to be about branded destinations, which include social networks. What do I mean by branded destinations?

The Motley Fool (fool.com) is a branded destination. The Fool Community (that's actually a page on the site) offers a variety of suggestions and advice from community members covering everything from investment strategies to food and drink, financial planning to health and fitness. Members of the community, who must register to participate, can log on and ask for help. iVillage.com is a branded destination; Gather.com is a branded destination. I would even argue that any site, after it reaches a certain critical mass, can be considered a branded destination.

The next generation of branded Web destinations will be designed as a place to aggregate, supported by advertising. Look at Eons.com, founded by Jeff Taylor, who founded the Monster.com job site. Eons is sort of a MySpace for baby boomers. Members (and you have to be at least 50 or lie about your age to become a member) can share life dreams, calculate life expectancy, follow news stories about aging, and much more. The site carries advertising; recent ads included Royal Caribbean, Fisher Price, Liberty Mutual. People who clicked on the Fisher Price ad were linked to an online sweepstakes; by entering, they agreed to receive promotional e-mails from the company.

In addition, remember that the social web filters transactions. The Eons site is an example of this. People who jump to the Fisher Price sweepstakes site from the Eons site are prescreened; the odds are good that the majority are grandparents or indulgent aunts and uncles who would be interested in children's toys. Or consider eHarmony.com, "the first service within the online dating industry to use a scientific approach to matching highly compatible couples." Single members join to find a partner; married couples join to strengthen their marriages. People who visit the site can take surveys and buy relationship books.

These—and hundreds of other sites—are social interfaces that may lead to a transaction, versus sites that simply offer transactions, which is where the Web has been for the past 10 years. It is the difference between going to a site to buy things and going to a site for an experience and *then* buying. In the future, branding will be built more on experience and discussion about the experience, although traditional advertising and promotion will still have some influence. For some leading brands, the future is now. Dialogues about experiences are already shaping and reinforcing what community members think, feel, say, and do about these brands.

Ordinarily it takes a long time to build a brand, but the social web has shown this is not always true. It took Google about eight years to become a verb. YouTube did not spend a dime on advertising and became a national brand in less than three years. iVillage has become a brand for information for women. MySpace, Friendster, BlackPlanet, Gather, and more have become brand names almost overnight.

How did that happen? Through the dialogue on the sites and the conversations visitors have with each other, the brands became strong. Not just dialogue but also the fulfillment of a promise made through that dialogue, either by offering information a visitor wants or by getting to the product through the information. Brands will become more and more powerful as they fulfill the promise made in their dialogues with customers and the dialogues among customers.

Any brand that tries to game the system or has a shoddy product or shady proposal will be found out more quickly and punished more severely on the social web. The "Wal-Marting Across America" blog, the super-duper Kryptonite bike lock (which someone discovered could be picked by a Bic pen and broadcast how on the Web), and the

"Dell Hell" service problems are just a few examples of how Web-savvy consumers can, and will, turn on a company they feel has not done the right thing.

Too Much of a Good Thing

As the social web grows and customers get on board, they'll vary their participation in what I see as three tiers of communities:

1. The first tier of communities are built around what customers talk most about, care most about—school, profession, disease, hobby, sports passion, dating service.

2. The second tier of communities are those that customers will visit now and then. These may not be as important or immediate as the first tier but they're of enough interest to warrant an occasional visit.

3. The third tier of communities are where customers go when they have something specific in mind. Maybe they're thinking about an annual vacation, a refinanced mortgage, a presidential election. Customers aren't always looking for travel tips, but when they're getting ready for their one big trip of the year, they might visit three community sites to look for interesting places.

A customer may buy many different branded products, but they'll only belong to a limited number of communities on the social web, perhaps 10 or 12. Moreover, many of these communities may have only marginal connection to commerce. Over time, people will most likely perform triage on their community involvement. Some will belong to subcommunities; they may not be directly in dialogue with the company, but will be comfortable with the company. For example, someone may trust L.L. Bean or Orvis and will continue to watch the company's site now and then or dip in and out of the community maybe once a month or so, just as shoppers like to drop into certain stores at irregular intervals.

Once the novelty of the social web wears off, people will become more selective. For example, Aarica Caro, a 28-year-old escrow officer who lives in Morgan Hill, California, has shared enough. She's shared a list of her favorite television shows and movies, reviews of Bay Area haunts, and she's been invited to share more. She was invited to join other online communities such as Yahoo 360, but she didn't bother to sign up. She said her MySpace page is enough. "It's getting pretty old," Caro said. "It makes no sense to have a million of those pages. I have one."

For a while, Caro shared the lives of her three cats on Catster.com. She kept an online cat diary for six months and each of her cats had about 50 online friends. "At that point, I thought, 'Who cares?'" she remembers. "Who cares if my cats have friends?" That's when she stopped writing about their adventures.[2]

So the question is one of engagement, which is all about content. How do you build relevant content that will get people coming, talking, returning to your site? How do you build the mix of professional user-generated, enterprise-generated content to do that?

Obviously, no one specific, concrete answer fits all situations. Companies and communities are far too diverse. The most I can do here is raise the issue and suggest some principles. I believe a good analogy is that of a brilliant magazine editor. The best editors understand their readers. They know what will interest, entertain, excite their readers; what interests the readers of Car & Driver is different from, say, what interests the readers of Skiing. True, the two magazines' readership may overlap somewhat; some skiers are passionately interested in cars. But faithful readers would be surprised to find an article about a new ski resort in Car & Driver or a review of a new convertible in Skiing. Enough said.

Ten Rules for Private Communities

Sometimes your best bet is to set up a private, invitation-only community for your conversation. This is the specialty of Communispace, which creates consumer, customer, and employee communities that companies can use for marketing insights. Diane Hessan, Communispace's CEO, tells me that Communispace obsesses over how to keep community members returning regularly. Why? If members don't participate, the community has little value to the sponsoring company.

Following are 10 principles that Communispace has developed from its experience with private communities. While they apply most specifically to that firm's business model, they can be adapted to other communities, particularly in a business context. Any company with salespeople, distributors, dealers, franchisees, store managers, or other natural groups in farflung places could profitably adapt these ideas:[3]

1. *Invite the right people, keep it private and small.* When you find people who have a common interest and put them together in a community, their energy explodes. Screen people to uncover interests, passions, and willingness to participate, and avoid using only simple demographic and geographic criteria. But keep the community private. More of the right people are likely to participate in private communities than in public communities because they feel more comfortable in an environment where they know what they say will only be seen by other identified community members, the facilitator, and company representatives.

2. *View members as advisors to the company.* Think of community members as valuable advisors to your company, not as a market research panel. When you treat community members as advisors they will go to amazing lengths to help your company—and for very little compensation. People in one of Communispace's shoppers' communities drove over 100 miles to check out and compare competitive stores despite high gas prices. An important note: Be sure to let your community advisors know how your company is using their ideas. The more you reciprocate, the more people will help you.

3. *Find the social glue, make it member-centric.* The more focused the community is on topics of shared interest and relevance

to its members, the more involved they are likely to be. Don't base a community on just your product or company. Rather, find the commonalities among potential members that are also relevant to your business, and ask people for help in better understanding that particular topic or domain. For example, one pharmaceutical client is exploring the emotions behind a disease and how people make treatment decisions rather than just testing drug ads. A financial services client is exploring not just how people feel about their brand or even their category, but how and why members have come to consider themselves consumer activists.

4. *Work at building the community.* Communispace has found that, on average, 68 percent of community members are actively participating within 48 hours of joining. One reason for such high participation is that the firm creates community-building activities to help people quickly understand what the community is about, make them feel comfortable participating, and help them get to know one another over time. Some of these community building best practices are creating "rituals" like Tuesday night chats or "random thoughts" weekly polls asking people to post personal profiles, share personal stories relevant to the community's focus, or upload photos, like pictures of their favorite pet or the inside of their medicine cabinet.

5. *Be genuine, encourage candor.* The community's facilitator should set a genuine, open, and candid style and tone for the community. When a new member starts a conversation, make a big deal about how much you value the comment because this will reinforce the behavior. For example, "Hey, great idea. We want to hear everything so please say what you want." Or the reinforcement can be a spontaneous award. Make a conscious effort to give people permission to be honest and say what they really think.

6. *Just plain ask.* Companies often over-think how to phrase a question or issue to community members. The best way is to

just ask in a simple, straightforward manner. One client came up with a dozen ways to try to understand why African Americans didn't use their products. Communispace suggested just asking African Americans flat out: "Why?" A retail client was worried about customers' reactions to a number of store closings. The best advice: Post the press release and ask members what they have to say about the closings. Another technique that is quite successful is to ask members: "What are we missing? Is there something we didn't ask about that you wanted to share?" Members almost always say something useful.

7. *Pay even more attention to what members initiate.* While companies regularly poll members and ask them to take brief surveys and answer questions, the best insights often come from discussions started by members. How members talk to each other about how an issue or product "fits" into their lives can be incredibly revealing, as is how members influence one another. Within 24 hours of launching an investment community, for instance, 11 different dialogue topics were underway and only 4 of those had been seeded by the community facilitators. Members created the rest around issues they cared about. The lesson: Listen more than ask.

8. *Don't squelch the negative.* One of the most common mistakes marketers make is to try to squelch conversations about negative feedback. "We can't let them talk about that!" is a common reaction. However, some of the best lessons come from hearing about those things that annoy, disappoint, or outrage customers. Encourage members to give the good, the bad, and the ugly.

9. *Don't ask too much, too often.* As marketers get to know their community, many become overly enthusiastic about the ability to ask customers all the time, any time, about everything—new product ideas, advertising concepts, competitor moves. Don't ask members for too much too often or they will become fatigued.

10. *Use the right mix of technologies and methodologies, and keep experimenting.* Make sure the community is built on multiple underlying technologies and methodologies so that people aren't stuck just answering surveys or posting to message boards, and so you can mine the insights with the right analytics. Engage members through a variety of functions: conduct live chats, create visual member profiles, use icons to classify discussion replies, upload advertisements; ask members to review products, keep diaries. Communispace recommends blending a range of methodologies and modes of expression including ethnographic, storytelling, mystery shopping, role-playing, video diaries, and polling. Similarly, keep experimenting with ways to more deeply involve people, create a richer community experience, and analyze what the community's conversations mean to marketing strategies.

"The primary reason that people don't belong to a community is because they don't think it will be worthwhile," says Diane. People don't usually leave a community they've joined, but their participation may drop. Software can track member participation, and when there's a dropoff, Communispace will send a note: "Hi, how are you doing? What is going on? We see that your participation has dropped."

Many of the reasons why participation drops have nothing to do with the value of the website. Sometimes members get really busy, or a message may have been screened out by their spam filter, or they experienced technical problems getting into the site. "Given that our communities are pretty intimate," says Diane, "we have phoned participants to talk about this. If we think we have the right person and we are doing the right things, we want to know whether there is something we can learn for other communities. Can we do something differently to capture their imagination?"

What if someone doesn't respond and doesn't participate? "Because we have private communities," says Diane, "we control whether people are allowed in. If they are not participating, we replace them, because we have limited space. We don't take it personally. We just say this is somebody who is not interested and we are going to give somebody else that seat."

How Do You Pay for It All?

At some point, company management has to think about the expense of creating and maintaining a community. Where is the money going to come from to pay for this? I argue that a lot of this can be done inexpensively with existing website templates, a digital camera, and a little imagination. A small or local business—a restaurant, craft workshop, specialty toy store—can build a community around its content and include customer reviews and discussions. This lets visitors click into the conversation.

Larger companies may have to shift money from other budgets like television advertising—a movement that is already underway. Among the *Fortune* 500, the real money has to come from the more than $90 billion these companies spend on television. Let's assume that consumers are avoiding roughly 20 percent or more of all commercials. (We'll know better when Nielsen is able to report its measurement figures.) Do the math: 20 percent of $90 billion is $18 billion. Taking a fraction of the national television advertising budget and devoting it to community building could have a far greater effect on the brand. Moreover, it could actually determine the effect because the social web is inherently measurable (as we'll see in Chapter 9).

Marketing on the social web will cost a large company far less and return far more than almost any other marketing activity. Paradoxically, you have to think like a really good television station of the past to be a really good purveyor on the social web. You have to be constantly thinking about content that will get people talking to one another and returning to your destination over and over. This is your opportunity to polish a reputation as a branded destination where visitors can have dialogues with other interested people. Go out to other people's parties, and also invite people back to your party. This is going to be an increasingly important shift in thinking as the social web expands.

Marketing budgets can be reduced and marketing departments can spend less time and effort in marketing to the social web. There's a bigger picture, too, if you look beyond the money angle. Earlier in this chapter, I mentioned that Stonyfield Farm embraced the environmental protection cause. How do you think its customers feel when they see the company investing to build a community and champion causes that could ultimately affect millions of people? Even if Stonyfield's causes aren't your causes, my point is that money can't buy that kind of brand reputation. So my last bit of advice about engaging communities in conversation is: Put your heart into it and think about the long term.

CHAPTER

9

Step Five: Measure the Community's Involvement

(Who, What, Where, When, Why, and How)

Do customer communities pay off? Throughout this book, I've argued that marketers must aggregate communities to reach and influence groups of people who share similar interests, concerns, or behaviors (or all three). This is not so different from the way companies currently define and segment their markets, except that they usually use demographics, which is a very crude tool for identifying prospective customers.

Now the social web can simplify the targeting task and make it more accurate because people identify themselves (by behavior and

111

interest) according to the communities they join. But do communities really pay off? Research suggests that the answer is yes.

René Algesheimer, an assistant professor of marketing at the University of Zurich, and Paul M. Dholakmia, an associate professor of management at Rice University's Jesse H. Jones Graduate School of Management, designed a year-long field experiment to find out. Collaborating with eBay Germany's managers, they identified 140,120 active eBay users, people who had bought or sold something on the site within the past three months but had not participated in eBay's online communities before.

Algesheimer and Dholakmia randomly selected 79,242 customers and invited them via e-mail to participate in eBay's customer communities at the beginning of May 2005, offering them prizes such as iPods as an incentive to do so. The other 60,878 customers, who were not invited to join, served as the control group. So what happened?

"Within three months, 3,299 of the invitees became active community participants, posting messages, joining in discussions, and helping other members," the researchers report. "We call these customers the 'community enthusiasts.' An additional 11,242 users became 'lurkers,' reading others' posts without actively participating in the communities themselves." But what about their behavior?

The researchers say they were astonished at the differences between the two groups: "Lurkers and community enthusiasts bid twice as often as member of the control group, won up to 25 percent more auctions, and paid final prices that were as much as 24 percent higher, and spent up to 54 percent more money (in total)." Enthusiasts listed more items and their monthly sales were as much as six times higher than the control group's sales. Just as impressive, nearly ten times as many lurkers (56 percent) and enthusiasts (54 percent) started selling on eBay after they joined the customer communities.

For eBay itself, the increased activity of enthusiasts and lurkers "generated approximately 56 percent more in sales during the year that our experiment ran than in the previous year," Algesheimer and Dholakmia observed. "With a take rate (the fraction of sales that eBay earns as revenue) of 10.3 percent and a gross margin of 82 percent, eBay earned several million dollars in profit from the increased trading behavior of the community participants in the experiment. Our results show that customer communities pay off handsomely for eBay and suggest that any online company will benefit from nurturing its communities."[1]

On the Path to Payoff

Long before you start to measure the payoff—in fact, before you actually implement any community initiative—you should clarify your objectives for marketing to the social web. You might aim for marketing objectives such as:

- Improving customer relationships
- Improving channel relationships
- Building market share
- Building brand awareness
- Inducing product trial

In addition, your financial objectives might include:

- Boosting sales revenue from specific goods and services
- Improving marketing return on investment

And you can certainly use marketing to the social web for societal objectives such as:

- Building awareness of and involvement in charitable or civic activities
- Increasing awareness of specific issues (energy conservation, environmental protection, and the like)

Before you jump on to the social web, be clear about what you would like to accomplish . . . and what measure(s) you'll use to determine your progress toward reaching your goal(s). In fact, it's important to know *exactly* what you want to measure before you build whatever it is you're going to build. Before you write a single line of code, before you approve any creative, you need to plan what you want to measure, how you're going to do the measuring, and how often.

Remember, however, that your objectives and measures must take into account the *users'* experience, which is what communities are all about.

For example, say your goal is lead generation. Typically, management may say, "We need to measure conversion at each point in the user path." Applying this to a social web situation, your management would want to know that user number one entered the site. I'll call him Larry (although, of course, you won't know names at this point). They also want to know that Larry moved through the low barrier registration—that he gave a user name and picked a password . . . downloaded the case study in the site's low barrier area . . . submitted the additional information needed to gain admittance to the next tier . . . that he went to the next tier and that he completed a form giving the company his phone number or e-mail or more.

All that is very possible to do, and it suggests that Larry will be a very dedicated browser, but you have to think through the value proposition. Is Larry really going to want to give the name of his first-born child for the honor of providing the company with his e-mail address? This is a common blunder that companies make all the time. I know of one company site where you almost literally have to give your mother's maiden name just to download a case study that demonstrates the firm's capabilities. Sure, the firm is able to measure visitor movement every step along the way, but by doing so it sets up hurdles that defeat another goal: to have as many visitors as possible downloading the company's material.

Users will give you information to the extent they think they are getting something of value in return. This is why you can't lose sight of the user experience. Your company's perception of value is not going to be the same as your users' perceptions. Senior managers may demand all kinds of conversion numbers before they fund the site, but at end of the quarter they'll have only a handful of leads if they put up too many barriers. Which do you want? The measurements or the leads? Think about it.

The One-Two Punch

Once again, when you're considering community measurement issues, don't forget what you already know. Online measurement challenges are similar to the kinds of challenges you'd face in direct marketing, marketing communications, or advertising. If, for example, you're in marketing communications, how do you measure activity now? If you're an advertising manager, how do you measure ad impact today?

I'm very well aware that we're operating in an era of accountability. Nowadays, chief financial officers want to know the return on the marketing investment just as they want to know the return on a new building or a new bulldozer. As *BusinessWeek* wrote: "For years, corporate marketers have walked into budget meetings like neighborhood junkies. They couldn't always justify how well they spent past handouts or what difference it all made. They just wanted more money— for flashy TV ads, for big-ticket events, for, you know, getting out the message and building up the brand."[2]

So there is a convergence between what management wants and what the social web in theory is able to deliver. But let me ask another question: Do companies stop buying television time or print space because they can't measure, with real precision, the connection between media advertising and sales revenue? Obviously not. Instead, American companies have settled on measurements, like gross rating points (GRPs) or cost per thousand (CPM), that relate to factors that syndicated research companies, like Nielsen, Arbitron, and MRI, can measure. Those measures enable outlets to sell their advertising space in a way that feels fair enough for the advertisers who buy them. Yet they're not really measuring the medium's effectiveness. When you think about it, GRPs have very little to do with measuring your marketing effort's effect.

Still, that doesn't mean you should stop buying television time. Depending on your product or service, your size, and your financial requirements, you probably do need to build some awareness, which you can do using various types of paid advertising. However, even companies that have little or no television or print advertising can be successful.

YouTube.com is a good recent example—no paid awareness-building yet, but it was purchased by Google for $1.65 billion.

At the other extreme, the marketing literature is littered with examples of companies that spent millions of advertising dollars and obtained virtually no awareness. Let me also note that where advertisers *can* measure the advertising's effect—in newspaper classified advertising, for example—the Web has had a major impact.

I see marketing on the social web as packing a sort of one-two punch, even though there are no cut-and-dried answers to "What should I measure on the Internet and how?" One punch is the digital media marketing piece, in which you build content that is relevant to your marketing goal. This could be awareness, leads, sales, or some other marketing objective. The second punch is inviting people to participate in, be informed by, or be entertained by that digital media experience.

This one-two punch of the social web combines two marketing areas. You might, for example, use it for interactive marketing in arenas where you're not paying for media placement. (I'm not talking about banner advertising or popups or other intrusive paid ads.) Or you might use the social web like traditional public relations, in which case you can use Web analytics as you would on the corporate website if you've set up the content properly to capture the data.

It's All about the Data

E-tailers sweat bullets and spend millions on tracking software to make sure they know absolutely everything about the paths users take through their sites so they can optimize the browsing and buying experience. This is a little like (but much cheaper than) following customers through the store, observing the departments they visit, see which displays grab their attention, seeing where they spend the most time, and recording what they buy.

If your company is not an e-tailer, you probably don't need to spend quite that much on Web analytics or spend so much time designing your site to trace a visitor's path. Still, you should look at certain things, depending on your objectives.

If your objective is awareness generation or even better, consideration in the purchase cycle, you may want to measure time spent on the
site. A number of clothing sites and e-tailers, such as H&M, Levi
Strauss Signature, Adidas apparel, Land's End, and Speedo United
States, invite visitors to configure sophisticated virtual models to
their body type so they can see how the apparel will look. Think how
this will impact the user experience—and how much more time visitors are likely to spend on a site where they can get a sense of what the
clothing will look on *them*.

Another example is car configuration sites that let visitors mess
about with vehicle options, color, and more. A third example would
be the consumer electronics hardware sites where visitors can configure their own computer. This last may not be as visceral an experience
as trying on clothes or looking at car models, but it is one way to get
people to spend time on the site and get involved with the product.
You want to see how well the eventual product is going to meet whatever need brought a visitor to the site in the first place. Once visitors
have invested time on your site, hopefully they will either buy from
you online (if you're Dell) or contact a dealer for more information
and a price quote (if you're General Motors).

If you plan to use the site for lead generation, you'll need ways to
measure different things. Where, for example, do visitors come from?
Ads on Google or Yahoo? A blog? The link at a partner's site? Set up
your site so you can measure conversions at each step in the process
without diminishing the user experience. If we build a microsite as
part of our social media marketing program, we are going to do the
same as if it were a pure lead generation site. The ultimate measure, of
course, is the number and quality of the leads generated by the site.

Or suppose your company wants to reach as many people as possible. On the Web, you can measure how many unique visitors come to
a site during a day, a week, a month; further analysis will help you determine what provokes a flurry of visits.

Measuring digital media relations is not so different from traditional public relations in the sense that you're using measures to evaluate the quality of the coverage you get. Yes, you count the hits
(quantitative), but you care more about one outlet versus another outlet

(qualitative). So digital media relations allow a qualitative and slightly quantitative ability to measure the results.

In fact, if you set things up properly on the digital media marketing side—and *only* if you have set things up properly—you can use what are now traditional Web analytics to measure the results: share of voice, share of market, evidence of and quality of community, and cost of market share.

Share of voice is very similar to what you'd measure in traditional public relations. If your organization aspires to leadership in your industry, you have make your voice heard. Be available to respond to editors and reporters from the *Wall Street Journal*, the *New York Times*, *BusinessWeek*, and the trade press who call for comment. You also initiate discussions about issues You don't hide in your office.

Share of voice is about thought leadership. It goes back to my point that a brand is only as strong as the dialogue it has with customers. If you have more powerful ideas and content on the social web, then you're going to have a greater share of the dialogue than your competitor. The more you can explain and promote what has made you successful in a compelling and engaging way, the greater your share of voice.

For example a number of technology companies host a forum for customers, chief information officers's, in the healthcare industry. Hosting such a meeting where one of the technology company executives asks the questions creates a share of voice on its turf. If you mix professional and customer-created content by inviting a magazine editor or a well-known author who fits that niche or subject matter to you can attract, engage, and keep people coming is an excellent way to obtain share of voice.

Share of market is about marketing to the social web to secure share in priority markets at a faster rate and lower cost per lead than you'd typically get with traditional media. An immediate objective of lead generation should, ultimately, move the company to a goal such as increasing market share profitably.

Here's a hypothetical example. Suppose a company I'll call Intergalactic Software (or IS) sees as an opportunity to expand lead generation activities in a specific vertical market that is currently underserved. Intergalactic Software's marketing department creates a microsite to generate leads and promotes it using digital media relations. In other words, IS wants to increase share in that particular vertical market using social media marketing. Intergalactic Software may not be able to determine exactly how many points of market share it's captured because of the microsite, but, then again, it may be able to. If the company has incremental sales that it can trace back to leads generated by this social media marketing, the site will have affected IS's share of units and dollars in that market.

Evidence of and Quality of Community

This is a somewhat qualitative measure, based on the premise that engaging your constituents, customers, partners, or prospects is a good thing. If you believe that having quality interaction with and between your customers is a good thing for thought leadership, awareness generation, or for innovation is a valuable activity, then the case is made. If you don't believe this—or, more likely, you don't believe the effort is worth the return—then you won't care about the evidence and quality of the community.

In many cases, a key goal of marketing to the social web is to learn, quickly, how your customers want you to improve your products and services. Assume that, in fact, you've set a marketing goal of generating new product enhancement ideas. You could build your community to encourage participants to generate ideas and then you'd count the ideas you actually get. For maximum accountability, measure from idea generation all the way through the product pipeline to see how many and which ideas are actually implemented—and how they fare with customers.

For example, when Kraft Foods was looking into new dieting and healthy products, it consulted the Communispace online community it was sponsoring. Kraft asked online participants what diet food represented to them and how they made choices when they snack. The corporation learned that customers didn't feel they needed to deprive themselves or diet—what they really wanted was the ability to control how much they ate. This prompted Kraft to develop 100 Calorie Packs, a line of small, one-person bags of Oreos and Ritz crackers. The results were dramatic: In the first full year of sales, the product line rang up $100 million in revenues.[3]

Tapping your online community for product ideas is a great goal, but there's more. Let me quote Joe Lichtenberg, vice president, business development at Eluma, a Massachusetts software company with a vested interest in online communities. Reacting to a *BusinessWeek* article about online communities, he posted this comment on BusinessWeek Online: "Clearly a great opportunity for companies to get real feedback and advice, but I think what was missed was that these types of communities can be the holy grail for marketers: 'A person like me' has become the most trusted source for information about a company or product. Marketers would do well to create an environment for their customers to interact—and we're chock full of Web 2.0 tools to make it happen. When marketers think about how to leverage social networking in their marketing initiatives, it should look like more this—a place for interaction and collaboration—and less like a corporate profile on MySpace!"[4]

In other words, once the community becomes involved (especially when it's a public community), others are likely to say, "Hey, that's a terrific idea!" You do risk getting a reaction like, "Well, that's about the most ridiculous idea I've ever heard in my life." But I would argue that just getting a reaction is good—better than being entirely ignored.

You might have noticed that consumer opinion on the Web tends to split widely over books, movies, music, indeed, most products. Look at the Amazon book reviews; they tend be written by people who either absolutely loved the book (perhaps because they're related to the author) or loathed it. Someone who is simply indifferent won't bother to say anything. It's people who have an interest one way or the other who are going to take the time and energy to voice their opinions—that's evidence of community.

It's Not All Milk and Cookies

Because the social web is inherently measurable, and because it's growing so rapidly, companies that offer Web analytics are also growing. According to Jupiter Research, a New York market research firm,

Web analytics software and services will zoom from $565 million to $931 million 2009.[5] As the demand for online measurement tools has grown, companies have responded. Google, for example, offers nine Publisher Tools for website owners to use in analyzing a site's traffic, increasing traffic, and adding interactivity. The Yahoo Publisher Network offers similar tools. Also, a number of independent companies offer measurement tools, including Ominiture.com, Coremetrics.com, WebTrends.com, and WebSideStory.com.

Still, it's not all milk and cookies—there are real problems in what to measure, how to measure it, and what (if anything) the measurements mean. In an ideal world, you'd like to be able to measure the social interfaces in relation to the number of actual transactions. For example, suppose you offer a podcast and a discussion with your customers about, say, accounting software. You include a Q&A session with the editor from *Accounting Today* as a guest speaker. It would be great to know that your podcast produced a record number of requests for information and product downloads. At this writing, however, such a podcast's effect would be very difficult to measure.

The content I've been talking about in this book creates an information circus. When you market to the social web, you have many things going on at once (professionally generated content, user-generated content, interactivity, everything else I've mentioned in earlier chapters). Does this circus of social interaction really have the payoff of pulling people through to try things or buy things? I believe it does, and the research I quoted at the beginning of this chapter strongly suggests it does. But at this moment nobody has conclusively proved that it does. There is, unfortunately, no metric for measuring the effectiveness of the social interface.

High-profile sites such as YouTube and Facebook have been very effective in using social interface to attract vast numbers of people. Will they be effective in encouraging transactions? It's hard to know right now, although obviously Google's management believes that YouTube has—or will have—commercial value.

So there's plenty of room for improvement on the measurement side. I'm a bit amazed that the blogosphere doesn't have what I would call a media kit. In theory, a blog could study its readers (because it knows who they are), be able to say how many readers it has, and what their characteristics are. At the moment, such measurements are difficult but they may be possible in the near future.

Because the paid media world has decades of experience in measuring and monetizing what works and what doesn't work in proceeding to transactions, it could help the social web world improve measures for marketers. Accountability is crucial: Companies want to validate that marketing to the social web is a powerful way to attract and engage a potential customer.

Consider the example I used in Chapter 1 of Gillette's Scruffy Boy trying to convince young men that the unshaven look is not sexy. The site is a lot of fun, cute, and sexy. But if the CFO at Gillette asks, "What effect has it really had on our sales?" I suspect that making a clear connection between Scruffy Boy and Gillette razor sales will be very difficult. Rather, I believe, Gillette believes that changing customer attitudes will help sales, since Gillette has 70 percent of the razor business.

Do you even need precise measurements? My associate Cinny Little tells me that by simply exploring a website, she can usually sense whether it was effective at achieving the company's marketing goal, if she can even figure out what their marketing goal was. "If I think the site was ineffective, I will tell you who had too much power sitting around the table—the marketers, the creative people, or the technology folks," she says. "If there seems to be a good balance between those three parties, the site was probably effective."

Catalytic Consumers

Nevertheless, with social web analytics, companies can learn things they either could not learn before or could not learn as quickly and economically. Consider what's happening at Compete Inc., an online consumer market research company.

Compete has permission from more than two million people to ask them questions and to observe their behavior online, with the goal of helping marketers improve their products and better satisfy customer needs. CEO Don McLagan tells me that his company can identify trends very quickly because a growing number of these two million people go online to research their options before they open their wallets or sign on the dotted line. "They look at a car online before they buy it," he says. "They examine multiple wireless systems before they decide on one. They look for home equity loans from sources other than the place they have a checking account."

By observing the online behavior of these people, Compete picks up on patterns and gains insights that help marketers make key decisions. Don described how, for an automotive client, Compete evaluated reaction to General Motors' "Everybody Gets the Employee Discount" promotion. "When something like that breaks you would like to know immediately—if not sooner—whether you need to respond, if you're a marketing executive at Chrysler or Ford or Toyota or Honda," he explains. "Should you use a similar promotion or can you respond selectively on particular models? Obviously, you'll eventually know what happened because the states register car sales and the documents are a public record, but by that time it may be too late for an effective response."

Two weeks into the first month of the General Motors promotion, says Don, "We saw the behavior of people online and we knew that the entire GM line was not being affected. We knew Hummers, trucks, and SUVs were being moved, but we also knew sedans were not being moved. Cadillac and Buick were not being moved at all and, to the extent there was movement, it was in Chevrolet with the SUVs and trucks."

Armed with this information, rival auto marketing executives would be able to tell their management, "We don't need to offer employee discounts across the entire line." If Chrysler, for example, had this data, it would know that its popular 300 sedan would sell well without an employee pricing incentive. Do the math: a $400 employee discount multiplied by approximately 20,000 cars equals $8 million that Daimler Chrysler wouldn't forego in attempting to meet General Motor's challenge, if it had the right data to make the decision.

Compete's research suggests that 75 percent of all auto buyers now research their choice online. Don says these "catalytic consumers" have three distinguishing characteristics:

1. Catalytic consumers use technology to make information an everyday resource. They don't sit on the couch watching television with the family, absorbing uniform marketing messages. Rather, they filter the deluge of messages to find just what they need—and then shut out the rest.

2. Catalytic consumers know their value to marketers; it's hard to miss. These market-savvy consumers are looking for their piece of the action—through rewards programs, downloadable coupons and contests, and other online promotions.

3. Catalytic consumers know that they alone have the ultimate power—the power of their own permission. They control when to grant their personal attention, to which marketers, how often, and for what reward. This, in itself, is a very significant development.

If you were an automotive marketing executive with access to Compete's research, you wouldn't have to guess about the effect of the General Motors promotion. Says Don, "You know what sort of conversion GM normally gets out of its demand, so you are able to infer what is likely to happen in time to do something about it. You don't have to wait for the end-of-the-month sales results to make your decision on what you are going to do and be prepared." What a powerful payoff, indeed.

CHAPTER 10

Step Six: Promote Your Community to the World

(Get 'Em Talking and Clicking)

Because there are a bazillion websites on the Internet, how do you get people to visit yours? What if you invited a community and nobody came? Clearly, you have to promote your community just as you have to promote a new product or a new service. Compelling content is only the beginning. You have to use the social media to get people talking so they'll come to your community and get involved. Yes, you can use traditional advertising and direct marketing, but these efforts should be focused on sending people to your digital community to be informed, entertained, and heard.

Suppose, as an example, you were in charge of Gap's marketing; how would you promote your community to the world? The principles of promoting your community apply to both consumer and business-to-business markets (and small and large business alike), but the Gap is a familiar name, so I'll use it to illustrate a few ideas.

Mind the Gap

First, a bit of background. The Gap's target market is 18- to 30-year-old women and men. The company has other brands, as you know: its Old Navy brand targets 10- to 20-year-olds; Banana Republic targets 28- to 40-year-olds. Different brands target different audiences, so how could the Gap—just that brand—reach and influence its specific audience?

If I were the head of Gap's marketing and wanted to reach my market in a new, effective way, I would first identify the online communities in which my key constituents are active. Where do 20- to 30-year-old women and men go online? Let's say the people I'm particularly interested in reaching are new to the world of work, having just graduated college, and they need clothes at moderate prices. They want to look professional, but where do they go on the Web and what online activities do they participate in?

Research shows the guys I want to attract are into fantasy football sites. I know they visit ESPN.go.com and they may even be going to cooking sites for meal tips. I know that the women visit the various beauty magazine sites. How do I identify the bloggers who are talking about fantasy football and fashion (at the same time if not in the same place)?

I'll start by using the large search engines (Google, Yahoo, MSN, Ask). This generates a list of the top industry news sites, blogs, and communities relevant to the domain. To produce a more extensive and targeted list, I use other searching tools, such as Brandpulse, Technorati, Alexa, and more to find specific sites focusing on the individual keywords. Who is talking about Gap the most online? I do that by simply typing words like, "Gap," "The Gap," "Gap Clothes," "Gap

Jeans," "Gap Shirts," and more. In this way, I can identify sites and start to narrow the online community to the sites that talk about my brand the most.

Over the next month or so, I'll monitor these sites to see exactly what the bloggers are saying. I may find one was an anomaly; it mentioned Gap once in a flurry of posts and never mentioned us again. Another blogger might write regularly about how she mixes and matches her Gap clothes with accessories from other chains. Yet another might talk about where to find Gap jeans at a discount online, a site that talks about nothing but price cuts online and how to buy things at a discount.

Now I know that blogger Susie Style is really focused on fashion and mixing-and matching-with other brands. I know that blogger Johnny ESPN is focused on getting the best discounts for ties and shirts for work. With this knowledge, I can buy advertising in the community websites for *Cosmopolitan* and *Allure,* which appeal to 20- to 30-year-old women who want to discuss fashion and related concerns. I can advertise on the ESPN site or I can advertise on the fantasy football sites via Yahoo (or both) to reach the 20- to 30-year-old men.

Also, I can e-mail Susie Style: "I know you're writing about our clothes. I've been reading your blog. I like what you're saying and I want to get to know you. I notice you mix-and-matched our Gap blouse with a Banana Republic skirt. Did you know that if you get a basic black Gap top you can use it 16 different ways?" I use my real name and let her know I'm from the Gap—this is not surreptitious.

Transparency is, in fact, a key point: You have to be open about who you are and what you want. Think of the social web world as a cocktail party. When you go to a party, you introduce yourself and often learn something about where the other person lives, what he or she does for a living, and what interests that person. You don't pull out a presentation and start flipping through the pages, no matter how attractive a business prospect that person might seem. You don't do that because you're in a social environment, and that's the way bloggers tend to think about what they're doing. A blog is a social conversation that people have with people.

My hope is that Susie Style will write in her blog something to the effect of: "You know what? I heard from this guy Larry at the Gap today, and he gave me a tip on wearing a black shirt with this blouse and these pants." Johnny ESPN might write, "I was contacted, and Larry who says he's from the Gap says I can get 10 percent off if I tell 10 friends to buy Gap pants. Each of us will get 10 percent off if we get 10 people to buy those jeans I was talking about last week." The blogging world may be social, but a company can still offer incentives to good customers.

Back in the real world, what do I say when Gap's CFO asks me what all this will cost and how my marketing department plans to justify it?

I say this is a campaign. We're not going to write Susie Style and Johnnie ESPN once and stop. It has to be an ongoing investment— but a relatively small investment for a large return. We've found that a company can spend as little as $2,500 to $15,000 to set up this kind of program; space in a national magazine can cost 10 times as much.

And while my Gap example is only that (the company is not a client and I have no inside knowledge), the *Wall Street Journal* quoted Scott Key, vice president for Gap Inc.'s online division, as saying, "Because the cost of [e-mail] distribution is so inexpensive, you have the opportunity to tailor messages. The click-throughs and purchases go up dramatically when you give customers a message they care about, rather than just broadcasting to them."[1]

Now for a Real Example

For a real example of how to promote a community, consider ITtoolbox.com. This firm has created a growing community of information technology professionals since its founding in 1998. It now has 30 websites with over a million pages of community-generated content that provides practical IT information and is supported by advertising. I recently asked Dan Morrison, the CEO and cofounder with George Krautzel, how ITtoolbox got started and how it's promoted.

First things first, Dan says: "Before you can even begin to market your community, you have to have something that users are actually going to find appealing, a value high enough to encourage them to participate. If you don't have that, you can promote as much as you want and you're still not going to get any participation."

The IT industry was (and is) an obvious candidate for such a community, if only because it's evolving so quickly. The idea for the site came when Dan, as an independent IT consultant, was working on a challenging tech issue with a colleague. Having exhausted their shared knowledge on the issue—and with no other place to turn—the colleague opened a book to search for the solution. Dan then realized that a site where IT professionals could share knowledge would be an extremely valuable resource and would be heavily used once professionals tried it and came to depend on it: "The value we were going to provide was that we were going to help a knowledge-based profession share that knowledge."

With that as a premise, they designed and put up the website and began promoting it with the same tools they use today: word-of-mouth and search engine optimization. Once IT professionals tell their friends about the site, the friends tell *their* friends, and the word spreads. Search engine optimization (which I'll talk about in more detail in Chapter 12) is a good way to help people who are looking for information you have. Both word-of-mouth and search engine optimization are extremely powerful in the community information model—far more powerful in the online community model than in the traditional editorial model.

"As a community, we view ourselves as competing with the traditional sources of information, which have all been editorial-based—primarily trade magazines and newspapers," says Dan. "In our case, the IT market historically has gotten all of its information through editorial processes, where a group of editors and writers create the information and then push it out to users in the publisher's chosen format."

While some communities on the social web are a mix of professional and member content, ITtoolbox users determine what topics they want to talk about and they create the content. That's the fundamental distinction between an online community and the traditional editorial model. And the online community model for an information website, Dan points out, is very conducive to viral growth, word of mouth, and search engine optimization.

The Little Website and How It Grew

To show how to promote an online community, let me use ITtoolbox as an illustration.

Dan had been an IT professional; he'd worked at Ernst & Young and Deloitte, and had contacts in the industry. When ITtoolbox was launched in 1998, it was primarily a discussion forum for certain IT topics, along with links to relevant sources. Dan was excited to tell his contacts about this new service: "Guys, go check this out." They started using it, and very quickly Dan and George added some proprietary community tools to the forums. "We put it out and we got a little bit of usage, but we did something else," says Dan.

At the time, many people were using Yahoo to find websites. In fact, they were using the human-edited directory more than they were using the search engine. Even if they were searching Yahoo they ended up searching the human-edited directory rather than what we think of today as a search engine index. "We got listed in Yahoo" says Dan, "and we found ourselves listed in AltaVista and as soon as that happened, traffic spiked. We had up to five hundred visitors a day for some of the IT knowledge-sharing websites. That was a really big spike. By getting that response, we were able to start building a critical mass of people who could then produce content."

What feeds search engines—and this is where communities are very, very good for the search engine model—is content, which communities generate in very high volumes. ITtoolbox is a phenomenal example of high volumes of very specific content that only gets more voluminous as community members answer questions and comment on the answers. That high volume of granular content is search engine food. The more you have, the more likely you are to show up in someone's search results.

A community like ITtoolbox, where users create around 1,500 to 2,000 pages of content every day, has very granular content compared to the traditional media sources, which produce perhaps a few dozen pages of content per day. (And that would be for a fairly well-established media entity, because researching and writing is a timely and costly process.) At ITtoolbox, the thousands of community members have already done the research and are generating thousands of pages of content, day after day after day.

Another reason that communities fit so neatly into the search model is because of the evolution of search itself. Early on, people would search for a simple key term, then go to the website and start checking out its content. Over time, they began searching using more complex key phrases. These days, people use search engines to search for a specific type of or piece of information. As a result, having high volumes of very granular content is very conducive to drawing traffic to the community (in other words, promoting it). In fact, this search model is becoming the primary way that people use the Internet.

Searching brings new people into communities and as they become participants, they begin to create content—which leads to even more search engine fuel. It's a very synergistic model of people creating high volumes of content that is a very potent draw for search engine traffic.

Another key point: ITtoolbox is open to the public. Nonmembers can get into the site via Google, Yahoo, Ask, or other search engines. But the community also has its own search engine, so that a member with a specific problem can search within the site. Dan and I believe that even a member-only site needs a mechanism by which members can search within the site.

Dan makes another important point about online communities: "If users can't find the exact information they are looking for, they can generally get the community to generate it for them by participating." What happens is people tend to search and to find something, but that often generates another question or an extension of the original search. As soon as people want to interact with the community to get value, they should become members and provide information about themselves. What information they provide depends on the community sponsor's marketing goals and, as noted in the last chapter, may be nothing more than a user name and password.

Again, ITtoolbox's content is freely accessible. Yet the members' active participation adds value, because they are able to obtain information that is specific to their unique needs. They must become an active participant to request the community's help in acquiring that information—which builds the community and feeds successive rounds of positive word-of-mouth.

One Size Doesn't Fit All

Unlike a magazine or newspaper (or a television show or movie, for that matter), says Dan, it's challenging to build a prepackaged user experience in online communities. Remember, it's relatively easy for the traditional editorial media, which produce fewer pieces of highly researched content, to create a prepackaged user experience. In an online community, however, members are producing tons and tons of very specific content—and as the content gets more narrow and specific, the potential audience for each piece of content grows smaller—hypertargeted. Within a community, it's quite difficult to create a meaningful prepackaged experience around such hypertargeted content.

"This is one of the areas in which we're continually evolving," Dan notes. "Can we create some of our own prepackaged user experiences to introduce people to the content and help walk them through it to get to the right places?" ITtoolbox's answer was to create what it calls "knowledge bases." At this writing, it has 28 knowledge bases— focused websites that each bundle all the community interaction related to a single IT topic. ITtoolbox has a website for customer relationship management issues, for business intelligence issues, for databases, for visual basic programming, and so forth. These serve as a sort of prepackaged user experience to showcase the type of content that the community is creating. They also provide a navigation path so visitors can find specific content. And, of course, they're one more way to promote the community to potential members.

Now online communities like ITtoolbox can create a user experience built around individual members, a sometimes overlooked technique that's becoming more commonplace. "We introduced a social network into our community," explains Dan, "to allow users to create their own online profiles. Then they can link to others, similar to the concept of friends on MySpace. Because the goal of our network is to help people share information, we want to help members find people who have similar needs so they can exchange information. And as they share content, they're creating content that can be reused."

The social networking feature on ITtoolbox puts users at the center of the experience (and gives them another valuable benefit to mention to potential members). Here's how it works. Say that Alpha, a member, has identified 30 people with similar skill sets and with whom he wants to share information—and these people are all active participants in the community. If Alpha connects with those people on the profile page at ITtoolbox, he'll see all the content those people post. I'll talk more about this in Chapter 11, but you can already see how this feature would excite members and attract newcomers—promotion just by innovating for the community's benefit.

Outside Expertise

An entire industry of specialist companies has sprung up to help if you choose to go outside for expertise in promoting your community. Type "search engine optimization" into Google and you'll get more than three million results, with eight advertisers and three sponsored links (today, anyway). Google itself offers a wealth of free advice, but many consultants and agencies are ready to help. Interestingly, the company at the number 100 spot in my current Google search is an Orange County, California, firm, WebPublicitee.com, that specializes in search engine optimization (SEO). A skeptic might wonder why there are 99 SEO results ahead of it. On the other hand, it's not at the number 1,000 spot.

GetMeVisitors.com promises to deliver traffic to a website in a slightly different way. Its website says: "We purchase abandoned and expired domain names that still have traffic. We make sure that these domain names fit into one of our categories. We work at a basic level by redirecting the traffic coming to these websites to your website if it falls into the same category. Once you order a campaign, one of our senior consultants will take a look at your site and analyze the category further to facilitate delivery of the most relevant redirected visitors. We make sure that the targeted traffic keeps pouring into your website, so that you keep using our services."[2]

Another company, Baynote.com, says it improves search results and thereby promote websites by connecting "your Invisible Crowd— the anonymous collection of website visitors that come to your site each day—allowing them to help *each other* on the website." Baynote's CEO Jack Jia told *PC Magazine Online*, "It's basically using the wisdom of the community to refine search results. Until recently, the focus of the Web was on producing content, but today's Web is decidedly about consuming content. An effective Web-based customer experience is the core of all online sales and marketing efforts, yet organizations struggle with how to guide visitors to the information that drives purchasing behavior."[3]

Multimedia Outreach

Other ideas about promoting your community: This is where I would use some traditional media. Every print ad you run should include your URL. The Super Bowl ads increasingly point you to a digital destination. Traditional media can play a role by helping direct customers and prospective customers to digital environments.

Another obvious idea is posting your thoughts, comments, reactions, or all three on other blogs. Go to other people's parties to let them know you have some cool things back at your party that others might want to come visit.

You can always promote your website the way companies have promoted themselves and their brands for years, with a contest. The social web, however, allows you even more options. For example, mainstream advertisers like Chipotle, Converse, General Motors, and MasterCard have invited consumers to create and post their own commercials on the Web. And as a symptom of how the line between television and Web is blurring, the CW network and Cadbury Schweppes developed a contest that involved the television show *One Tree Hill*, the Sunkist soda brand, and the Web.

The "Sunkist Brings *One Tree Hill* to Your Town Contest" invited viewers of the series to create videos and upload them to a special site (cwtv.com/Sunkist), where visitors then voted for their favorites. The winner's grand prize was a role in an episode to be filmed on location in the winner's hometown. "This is 360-degree marketing," said Bill Morningstar, executive vice president for national sales at CW, owned by CBS and Time Warner. "It starts on air, extends online and has the ultimate grass-roots layer, the show coming to the hometown." Sunkist first promoted the contest on an episode of *One Tree Hill;* visitors to the contest site also found promotions for CW shows, complete with schedules, video clips, and a "lounge" for posting comments about the series.[4]

Multimedia outreach is a great way to promote and build your community. Not long ago, Kellogg's and its agency, Brigandi and Associates, rolled out an ongoing, integrated campaign for Special K cereal that combines television and print advertising, couponing, point-of-purchase displays, and a variety of social web tools. The target audience is women who want to manage their weight to look and feel great.

Marta Cyhan, vice president-worldwide promotions, says: "We spend lots of time with women and clearly recognized that weight management is a journey." Kellogg's community (www.specialk.com), the focal point of the campaign, is designed to support women on this journey. The site is chock full of advice on weight management plus useful tools like a BMI calculator. Users can share success stories, post bulletin board messages, ask for support e-mails, and take pop quizzes to test their knowledge. With more than 100 pages of interactive content and seasonal weight-management themes, the site is a community for building relationships with and among customers.[5]

Kellogg's promotes the community through partners like *Shape* magazine; store displays and packaging that highlight the seasonal challenge and the online community; print ads in parenting and fashion magazines; and extensive television advertising during shows that draw a large female audience. "Integration is the key to consumer engagement," observes Kellogg's Cyhan. "The goal of promotion is to build the brand while motivating consumer interaction."

Best of all, the community has moved the needle on sales while attracting record numbers of new and return users. Sales of all Special K cereals have registered significant growth during the campaign, blowing past the company's forecasts for existing and new products.

Step Seven: Improve the Community's Benefits

(Don't Just Set It and Forget It)

Marketing to the social web is a journey, not a destination. It's a hike, not a camp out. It's a work in progress, not a statue cast in bronze. It's a . . . but you get the idea. You have to continuously improve the site and its value to the community. If you don't, you're liable to be MySpaced the way Friendster was.

What about Friendster?

Friendster wasn't the first social networking site. Back in the late 1990s, sites like Six Degrees and SocialNet came on the scene—and soon shut down. "We all basically hit the market before the market for social networking," says Reid Hoffman, the founding chief executive of SocialNet and now the founder of the LinkedIn social networking site.

But by the time Friendster, founded by Silicon Valley engineer Jonathan Abrams, hit the Web, the market was ready. "Basically, Jonathan wanted to meet girls," Silicon Valley entrepreneur Mark J. Pincus told the *New York Times*. Pincus provided Abrams with some seed money to finance the project at the end of 2002: "He told me himself, he started Friendster as a way to surf through his friends' address books for good-looking girls."

Friendster was up and running in March 2003. Without spending any money on marketing, it attracted three million registered users within six months. The media jumped on the phenomenon: *Time, Esquire, Vanity Fair, Entertainment Weekly, U.S. Weekly, Spin*, and other publications wrote about Friendster; Abrams even appeared on the late-night television talk show "Jimmy Kimmel Live." (He then boasted that Yahoo's founders had never been guests on that kind of talk show.)

As Friendster's growth exploded and it attracted investors, it also attracted a board of directors, mainly experienced venture capitalists and software executives who had little feel for the product. The board assessed Friendster's situation and concluded that Abrams was in way over his head; in April 2004, he was replaced as chief executive.

What happened? "All of a sudden, Jonathan had all these high-powered investors to please," Russell L. Siegelman, a partner at the venture capital firm Kleiner Perkins Caufield & Byers, told the *Times*. "He had all this money in the bank, so there was all this pressure to hire people and get things done. Open up new territories: China, Japan, Germany. Add all these new features. Meantime, he took his eye off the ball."

The ball, of course, was the site and the user experience. As Friendster became more popular, the site became slower, eventually taking as long as 40 seconds to download—an eternity and a half for its 16- to 30-year-old target market. Yet, according to insiders, such technical difficulties did not interest the board of directors; they were more concerned with potential competitors and new features, such as trying to add Internet phone services to the site.

Kent Lindstrom, who became Friendster's fifth president in the fall of 2005, says, "The stars would never sit back and say, 'We really have to make this thing work.' They were talking about the next thing. Voiceover Internet. Making Friendster work in different languages. Potential big advertising deals. Yet we didn't solve the first basic problem: our site didn't work." In retrospect, Lindstrom observes, the company needed to devote all of its resources to fixing its technological problems.

People inside the company realized they needed to add new features to the site if it was to compete with the new social networking sites, such as MySpace, Facebook, and Bebo. "There really wasn't much to do [on Friendster] once you set up your network and found your old friends," says Larissa Le, a former Friendster employee. Other social networking sites were adding features like blogs and tools such as video that people could use to customize their profiles. But at that point, adding new features to Friendster would only slow it even more.

Another problem was that competitor MySpace allowed its users' personalities to come through, whereas Friendster, with a smiley-face logo, had focused on safety and trust. For the most part, MySpace lets its members do what they want. "The key to MySpace is that it's controlled by the user," says Joel Bartlett, an organizer for People for the Ethical Treatment of Animals. PETA has space on both MySpace and Friendster; the MySpace site attracted 13,000 people, Friendster about 3,000.

MySpace, founded in July 2003, boomed: By the end of 2006, MySpace had more than 50 times the number of monthly domestic visitors as Friendster, according to comScore Media Metrix. Meanwhile, Friendster's venture capitalists reconstructed the board and hired another chief of engineering, who focused on performance and stability issues until Friendster performed as well as other social networking sites. Friendster also announced an instant messaging service and began featuring videos from YouTube and other sources.

These days Friendster, with 36 million members, hopes that it can position itself as a site for 25- to 40-year-olds who don't have the time or inclination to spend hours and hours on MySpace every day. The challenge now, said Lindstrom, is "to focus on a market for more than two months."[1]

Job One: Quality

Friendster's evolution has enough lessons for a marketing course. (Indeed, Mikolaj Jan Piskorski, an assistant professor at the Harvard Business School, uses the company as a case study in his strategy classes.) The first real lesson is: *Maintain your quality*. In a sense, what happened to Friendster is no different from what can happen in a manufacturing environment when a product suddenly catches on and, in an effort to fill orders, the company cuts corners. Very simply, as quality declines, customers defect.

Remember, customers look at quality in terms of how well your site meets their needs, expectations, or requirements. Ensuring that every link leads to the right place and every image loads perfectly every time is just the price of admission. To give your community a heartbeat, you have to look beyond mere functionality. The real question is: Does your site give customers what they want today—and what can you do to anticipate and deliver what customers will want tomorrow?

You just can't introduce a product or service and leave it unchanged forever. Look at Coca-Cola, a brand that's been around for more than a hundred years. Coke is always introducing improvements like new flavors, different size bottles, and variations such as diet Coke and caffeine-free Coke. A website requires the same kind of attention and constant improvement.

In fact, as soon as your website goes live, it's time to start improving it. Review your goal for each section of the site. How are you measuring whether you've reached that goal? Is that a true measure of success? For instance, are you attracting a high number of visitors but no one is downloading your white paper?

What action you would like each visitor to take? Is it easy for visitors to find what they want on your site? Here, you need input from a sample of actual target customers, not your own employees or people from the agency that handles your account. Does your content/functionality make it easy for visitors to take action? You (or your website designer) may think it's blindingly obvious that a red button labeled "Push Here to Download" means that a mouse click on the red button will initiate a download—but it may not be obvious to your visitors.

Every website of any size should have a clearly marked site map so that visitors can see how things are organized. And think about the way you list categories. For example, a tab labeled "Press" implies that the content will be articles in outside publications, whereas a tab labeled "News Releases" implies content posted by your PR or marketing people. (Sites do confuse these two, as I've seen in my surfing.) In addition to a site map, you might also consider a search engine for the site itself, something you can buy right off the shelf from Google and others.

A Case in Point

A company called The Complete Website (tcwebsite.com) features case histories that suggest various ways to improve a website. One of its cases focuses on six improvements designed to increase the number e-newsletter subscribers for Andrea Novakowsky, a personal and executive coach.[2] Here are they are:

1. Encourage visitors to your homepage to click the "Read the Latest Newsletter" or the "Read Our Tip of the Week" button. Don't put the signup on the homepage. Website visitors want to know what they're getting into before they give you their e-mail address. Be sure to position the e-mail subscription box close to the current newsletter. Also include text next to the newsletter or tip button that "sells/describes" the newsletter, white paper, or case studies you're offering.

2. Include a Tip of the Week page. TCWebsite says that after Andrea's homepage, this page is most popular.

3. Archive everything and provide an "Archives" link with the current newsletter. Archives increase your credibility.

4. If you have a testimonial or two about your newsletter, include it near your current newsletter, too.

5. Add a link to a Privacy Policy page so visitors can quickly and easily check your policy. For example, Andrea Novakowsky's Privacy Policy says, "We respect and are committed to protecting your privacy. We may collect personally identifiable information when you visit our site. We also automatically receive and record information on our server logs from your browser including your IP address, cookie information, and the page(s) you visited. Information Sharing and Disclosure: We will not sell your personally identifiable information to anyone."[3]

6. Add your signup form, a short newsletter description, and a link to the current newsletter on other subpages. No matter where visitors may navigate in your site, you should provide a quick way to find this type of content.

Peter Erickson, president of The Complete Website, writes: "Think about the approach as relationship building." Let's say a visitor hears about your business and looks for you on the Web. That person starts formulating an opinion of your business as soon as he visits your homepage. Make that first impression a good one, and you're on your way to establishing the relationship.

Most visitors will be reluctant to give even an e-mail address without a peek inside your site. The thought process of a visitor clicking through your site, says Erickson, probably goes something like this: "Hmm . . . 'Read our Latest Newsletter.' Well, newsletters are great insights into businesses since they cover current activities . . . so I'll bite and click into the news. A quick read and oh, yes the newsletter is great stuff! I might subscribe . . . still cautious. A Privacy Policy . . . that helps. A testimonial on the usefulness of the newsletter—wow, people seem to love it. Archives . . . impressive . . . look at all this content! This is serious. Hmm well I'm a skeptic but, what the heck, I can always unsubscribe, right?"

Clearly, the system works only when the content you offer is actually useful to your target audience—and you have to keep on offering new and useful content—but then you know that by now. Enough said.

Gather Ideas

Another way to improve the community's benefits is to extend the website's reach and impact. Here I want to focus on a few improvements made by Gather.com, a social networking site where members can connect with people who share their passions in books, food, gardening, health, money, music, politics, sports, travel, and more. Members can contribute thoughts, art, commentary, or inspiration and comment on other member contributions. One innovation involves a unique program with Amazon.com (a company that is itself a fascinating case history of constant testing and improvement). Amazon had introduced 49-cent Amazon Shorts, digitally downloadable short stories from published authors, both famous and unknown, who have titles available for sale through Amazon.com.

This improvement had unintended consequences that presented an opportunity for Gather.com. "Amazon's problem," Tom Gerace at Gather.com tells me, "was that it was turning away thousands of customers who were aspiring writers or very talented writers but who hadn't yet been published. As a result, these writers weren't eligible to participate in the Amazon Shorts program."

To address this situation, Gather implemented an improvement you can see at AmazonShorts.Gather.com. This is a writing contest, hosted on Gather.com, where unpublished writers compete to sell their short-form work on Amazon.com. Every month, Gather members can submit short works (2,000 to 10,000 words) and compete for four spots in the Amazon Shorts program. Gather members vote to choose three winners and the Gather editorial team picks a fourth winner. Winners have their work digitally published and sold through Amazon Shorts, moving from the ranks of amateur writer into the ranks of published author in a matter of months. "It's one of the ways in which we create strong community identification," says Tom, "and bring a benefit to the community through aspirational programs like this one."

Another way that Gather improved its community's benefits was to ally with Nintendo to offer an area on Games.Gather.com where members can play and discuss games. Tom explains: "We identified the top six game writers on our site by the quality and popularity of their writing, then sent them Nintendo game sets with no obligation. We said, 'Look, we're going to have a sponsorship from Nintendo. We're sending this to you because you're a respected authority on games. Check out this set from Nintendo if you like, and if you want, review it, and if not, don't. But please be transparent if you do review it, and let people know we sent you the game set so everybody in the community knows we're dealing above board.' We were reaching out and saying, hey, we respect your opinion and we really want your thoughts on the product."

Here's another improvement that Gather made, involving Mitch Albom, the author of *Tuesdays with Morrie*. To publicize his new book, *For One More Day*, Albom and his publisher had a tie-in with Starbucks and Gather to promote his readings and as a place for his blog about the book tour and the book. Members who visited Starbucks.Gather.com during "Taking a Book Break with Mitch Albom" could chat with Mitch online and post reviews of his books. This allowed Gather members to have a dialogue with someone they couldn't reach otherwise. "These are the kind of special events that improve the community's benefits," Tom points out. "You're creating tremendous value while also creating brand identification and brand definition for the community."

In planning improvements, your challenge is to dream up a game, a puzzle, an event, a cause, an issue that will make your site more valuable to visitors. Ideally the activity will connect to the brand, but not necessarily.

Gather gets the improvement process going by meeting with its agencies and partners to learn their strategic goals for the year. "We understand how they define their brand, who their target audiences are, how they're trying to reach those audiences, and what their key messages are," he says. "Then we work with them to develop 'wow' programs that benefit the community. We turn down programs we think will not create value, for two reasons. First, it will hurt the marketers and we don't want to create a bad experience for them. Second, it will hurt the community, and we're certainly not going to create a bad experience for our community. We'll only take programs that we think thousands of people will like."

The Improvement Imperative

A tech community, in particular, can never stand still, as ITtoolbox's Dan Morrison well knows: "We've been around for eight years as an online community, so we've seen a lot of evolution—from the Web 1.0 days of community to Web 2.0. Because online communities are a relatively new phenomenon, a lot of innovation is going on and you have to be prepared to change and improve."

Even if you're not running a tech community, you must be sure that your central focus is always on providing value to a meaningful community. By "meaningful," I mean the community should be large enough to produce some kind of value for the members and for you as a business. At the same time, you should have the community as the center of your world and keep it there, building the community around members' desires, not around yours (or your boss's).

And you have to continually introduce innovative improvements to remain relevant to your community. At ITtoolbox, Dan has two pieces of advice on how to do this:

1. *Listen to your users and respond to them.* They'll tell you what they want. You can try to get them to do something, but ultimately members are going to do what they want and participate only when they find value. If you're an astute listener, you'll find clues to new features that you *and* your users think are valuable. No matter how good your site is, your users can always suggest improvements. If you respond to those ideas—to

their desires rather than your own intentions—they will continue to grow the community for you.

2. *Be alert to new innovations and test them against the value you
   want to provide.* The whole idea of social networking wasn't
   even around—certainly wasn't very prevalent—just four years
   ago.[4] It started popping up and even then people weren't
   thinking about it in the professional sector. A savvy community operator constantly looks around for what's new and then
   thinks through the implications and possibilities.

Ask yourself constantly: What changes have occurred on the Web
and in the industry, and how might those apply to me? Some changes
may not seem relevant at first glance, but don't be too quick to dismiss
something. For example, Dan remembers that when ITtoolbox
launched a blog function in 2003, people viewed blogs mainly as opin-
ionated personal journals. Blogging was a successful phenomenon in
some parts of the social web for consumers, but would it translate well
in the business-to-business world and provide quality content?

ITtoolbox persisted and dug deeper, Dan says: "Could a blog help
IT professionals share information in a well-structured, predictable
way? Yes, it could. If so, what would the program look like?" The company developed a structured blog program where members could (and
did) post their daily experiences. A day in the life of a chief technology
officer . . . a day in the life of a chief information officer . . . a day in
the life of a security administrator. Suddenly ITtoolbox found members sharing very specific, very targeted information through a blogging platform, not something people were generally doing at the time.

Because ITtoolbox is all about helping people share information,
blogging added value to the community. The blogging platform "has
been very, very successful for us. We still have 300 percent year-to-
year growth in our blogs program." Dan says.

Recently, the site introduced a social network into the community. The new feature allows members to create their own online profiles and link to others, a la MySpace. How does this add value? Say a
member identifies 30 active ITtoolbox participants with similar skill
sets and with whom they would like to share information. The mem-

ber connects with these people on his or her profile page and can then see all the content posted by the linked members. Not only can the member customize the profile and the experience, the chain grows as the linked members share information with still other members.

This improvement is extremely powerful because it puts users at the center of the community and allows them to build an experience around the people they choose to communicate and share information with. As users post new information, it appears on their profile pages and simultaneously on the profile pages of the members with whom they're connected. In a sense, this improvement is creating minicommunities as members connect with other members who are important to them.

Another important point: Adding a cool tool to your community may be fun, but it's not the tool that counts. If you don't give users the value they want, it doesn't matter whether you add a wiki, blog, or the latest tech tool du jour. And Dan tells me that adding a single tool or feature may not be enough to deliver the value that a community expects or desires. Often you'll need a combination of tools, depending on the community, the average age of the members, and their interests and experience. So think about the value you're trying to provide and plan your improvements accordingly. If you have that mindset, it's a lot easier to continually innovate with the market (or maybe a little ahead of it).

Reality Check

You have an obligation to continually look for new innovations and figure out how they apply to your market—especially if you want to achieve or retain market leadership. If you don't, your site will become obsolete, more quickly than you'd expect because so much innovation is occurring in online communities right now.

After you've identified improvements you think will be valuable, you should get a reality check from your users: Here's what we're looking at, what do you think? How often have companies improved a product with features and benefits that the market cares nothing about? (The answer: They do it all the time.) *You* may think the website's new feature is wonderfully useful, but if your community doesn't agree, then the improvement will not add value.

Let me share an interesting example from the publishing industry. John Lawn, the editor-in-chief and associate publisher of *Food Management* magazine, announced in a recent issue that his publication wanted to provide a better search capability to help readers find posted articles online.[5] He also asked readers to give some direct feedback on the topics and search functionality they'd like to see on the site. Although not a complete cookbook for user feedback, a sample of his questions should give you food for thought:

- What kind of content from past issues of the magazine do you consider it important or useful to be able to access?
- What a kind of content that hasn't appeared in the magazine would you like to see in our online presence?
- What topics or categories of information would help you the most?
- Can you give an example of something you'd like to look for on our site, but can't easily locate now?
- What bothers you most about the way our site's information is right now?
- Which part of our current site do you visit the most, and why?
- What online product information would be most helpful to you on your job? One of our goals is to make a wider variety of past content available (right now, most of our site content only goes back two or three years).
- What specific kinds of articles from the past do you think should be our priority when it comes time to cull content from our archives for posting?

My last few words on the subject (and I can't say it too often): As technology and markets evolve, you can't simply create a site and leave it unchanged. If you don't regularly improve the community's benefits on terms that make sense to the members, your site could fade away.

Remember Friendster: At its low point, it still had millions of members, but most of them had not visited the site for more than a year.

You may not need (or want) more and more visitors, but you do want your members to come back often. The best way to bring them back is to constantly add new and different features or pages, add tools or information that make the site more useful, more interesting, more fun, or all three.

Making Use of the Four Online Conduit Strategies

CHAPTER 12

The Reputation Aggregator Strategy

(We're Number One!)

What, you ask, is a reputation aggregator? A site that provides rankings of content/sites. (I discussed reputation aggregators briefly in Chapter 7, in the context of online conduit strategies.) Reputation aggregators are a key—perhaps the key—gateway for most users to reach online content. People use these sites to decide what content they want or need when they're getting ready to buy, researching schools, looking up statistics, and so forth. Some popular reputation aggregators, ranked in order of total searches by a Nielsen/NetRatings report,[1] are: Google, Yahoo, MSN/Windows Live, Ask.com, My Way, EarthLink, Comcast, BellSouth, and iWon.

I call these sites reputation aggregators because, if you're going to search for anything, search engines like these aggregate the findings. They put sites or results or products in some kind of order—the most recommended or most linked or most used or bestselling or most visited, for instance. Because people can't buy your products or digest your ideas if they can't find you, you have to understand how search works and how it seems to be evolving.

Everybody Loves Search

According to a Pew Internet & American Life Project study, search engines are decidedly popular among Internet users. As the study's author, Deborah Fallows, wrote: "Searching the Internet is one of the earliest activities people try when they first start using the Internet, and most users quickly feel comfortable with the act of searching." Take a look at some of the study's findings:

- 84 percent of Internet users have used search engines, and on any given day, 56 percent of those online use search engines.
- 92 percent of those who use search engines say they are confident about their searching abilities; more than half, 52 percent, say they're "very confident."
- 87 percent of searchers say they have successful search experiences most of the time, including some 17 percent of users who say they always find the information for which they are looking.
- 68 percent of users say that search engines are a fair and unbiased source of information; however, 19 percent say they don't place that much trust in search engines.

Fallows noted that while people have positive feelings toward search engines, few are highly committed to searching. Most (67 percent) say they could return to the traditional ways of finding information. About one-third of the search engine users search every day, but most search infrequently; almost half say they search no more than a few times a week. Nearly all (93 percent) settle into the habit of using one or two search engines.

Now here's a particularly important point to bear in mind. Fallows found that while most consumers understand the difference between a regular television program and an infomercial, or between a magazine article and an advertorial, "only a little more than a third of search engine users are aware of the analogous sets of content commonly presented by search engines, the paid or sponsored results and the unpaid or 'organic' results." In fact, only about one in six searchers said they could consistently distinguish between paid and organic results.

"This finding is particularly ironic," she wrote, "since nearly half of all users say they would stop using search engines if they thought the engines were not being clear about how they present their paid results. Users do not object in principle to the idea that search engines will include paid results, but they would like them to be upfront and clear about the practice of presenting paid results."[2]

What Am I Bid for "Laptop"?

As the readers of this book know (even if two-thirds of the Americans who use search engines do not), paid search is where companies either bid on key words, or—growing more common—rent a word for a certain period. If you type in "laptop" on a major search engine, you're likely to see a number of "sponsored results" on the results screen. Google, Yahoo Live, and Ask all have a list of advertisers running down the right side of the results page. A recent list included BestBuy, ToshibaDirect, Sears, TigerDirect, Overstock, CircuitCity, and NexTag. These search engines also begin their list of results with several sponsored links, set off from the rest of the search results by a light blue tint. For the laptop search, these might include Lenovo, HPshopping, and SonyStyle.

In general, companies have a financial interest in being out in front where people can find them immediately. Why? Two reasons. First, my Google search for "laptop" turned up some 8,500,000 results—an unimaginably large list of results to wade through. Second, research shows that most people do not go more than three screens deep into a search. So if you are Lenovo, trying to build your brand name after buying IBM's PC business, it may be worth bidding high to be number one in Google's listings. You don't pay anything unless a searcher actually clicks on the link, and presumably the only reason people click is because they're shopping for a laptop. What do you have to lose?

On the other hand—one of the potholes on the information highway—there have been cases of click fraud, where unprincipled companies click repeatedly on a sponsored link to drive up a competitor's advertising expense. The search engines say they're aware of the problem and they're dealing with it, but you should also know about this issue when you think about search.

But does your brand or company really have to be number one in the result listings? There is, after all, a huge difference between someone who clicks through to your site and someone who actually buys your product. Every store has more browsers than buyers. You may do almost as well in terms of actual sales by being second or third or lower in the sponsored sites. Certainly you'll pay a lot less in advertising fees than the company in the top spot.

Also, if you turn up high enough in the organic search results, you may not have to pay anything. For example, in my "laptop" search, the first organic search site result on Google was "Apple— MacBook Family. Apple's official PowerBook product page with specifications, ordering, and other information" right under the three paid listings. Apple didn't have to pay for the spot, and would have wasted its money to buy an even higher spot.

Indeed, "bidding the highest amount for a keyword to ensure that your company tops the list of results may be a path to campaign failure," says Timothy Daly, vice president of marketing and strategy at SendTec, a St. Petersburg, Florida-based direct marketing services agency. "Recent research by San Francisco-based eye-tracking analysis software firm EyeTools, combined with what we see day in and day out with our clients, leads us to the conclusion that being number one in most cases is a waste of money, while camping out in a lower position often proves to be more productive."

Daly says that his agency commonly encounters a CEO or a vice president communicating downward to the search manager that "we want to be in the number-one position at all cost." And it goes the other way; the search manager wants to impress superiors and bids for the top spot without any regard for the relationship between cost and effect. No one in this common situation understands that the number-one spot is not always the best place to be.

"When two or three companies all have the 'top position' mentality," says Daly, "they almost always start a bidding war with each other, constantly raising bids until the top two or three bids are way out of tune with what's economically viable. Budgets are burned. Results are poor. And eventually, these bidders fall back to earth or disappear."

He observes that BlueNile.com, the wildly successful online jewelry company, announced it had pulled back on search because of this problem. "Unfortunately, you cannot control your competition," says Daly, "and in scenarios like the one BlueNile encountered, either these top-position bidders don't have the ability to measure return on investment for every keyword or they choose to ignore it."[3]

Web Marketing Today Free Weekly compared organic to paid search and concluded that organic search is more visible on the page; paid search is less visible except for the ads that appear above the organic search results. The full results of organic search may take several months to show up, whereas paid search's results take only several days.

That means it can be difficult for your firm to obtain a top position in an organic search's results listing; it's usually fairly easy, however, to buy the top position in the sponsored results if you're willing to pay the price. Finally, in organic search, traffic volume depends on the position for various key words and this can vary by search engine; in paid search, traffic can be high for all the important key words.

"Many novice marketers avoid using pay-per-click (PPC) ads," writes Dr. Ralph Wilson on *Web Marketing Today Free Weekly*, "because they're afraid it will cost too much. But in fact, PPC ads may be the only way you'll get any decent traffic to your site at all, unless you (a) have a rather noncompetitive business or (b) have optimized your website to rank high in natural search for the keywords important to you. The big advantage of PPC advertising is that you can get up-to-speed within a few days—the time it takes the editors at Google AdWords or Yahoo Search Marketing to approve your ads and keywords. Paid search may help you to generate a sufficient volume of traffic and sales to provide enough revenue to support your business."[4]

Bob Finigan, the vice president of product and marketing at Muzak, the venerable music provider, is now a believer in search. Until very recently, he says, Muzak had a skeleton website and no search strategy to speak of. Then the company hired Oneupweb, a Michigan agency specializing in search engine optimization and marketing. With Oneupweb's guidance, Muzak initiated a 100-word paid search program. Finigan says that within months, Muzak tripled the number of sales coming from organic and paid search. "We were able to put a program in place that is helping us dominate the Web space," says Finigan. The program is successful enough that Muzak bought 200 more words.[5]

Before you rush off to bid on key words, however, think about what WebSideStory found. Studying more than 57 million search engine visits to nearly 20 major business-to-consumer sites, this San Diego-based Web analytics firm learned that paid search has only a slight advantage over organic search in converting online shoppers to buyers. It also found that keywords bought on a PPC basis at search engines such as Google, Yahoo, and Microsoft MSN had a median conversion rate of 3.4 percent, compared with 3.13 percent for unpaid results to search queries.

"For both paid and organic search, you have highly qualified traffic that converts far above the overall conversion rate of about 2 percent for most e-commerce sites," said Ali Behnam, senior digital marketing consultant for WebSideStory. "In the case of paid search, marketers have better control over the environment, including the message, the landing page and the ability to eliminate low-converting keywords."

The study's results didn't discredit paid search. What they did show was that companies using online advertising should use a combination of available marketing tools, including banner ads, paid search, e-mail marketing, and search engine optimization techniques. "Most people don't understand that to get high conversion rates you need multiple touch points," said Rand Schulman, WebSideStory's chief marketing officer. "It's not just one or the other."[6]

The trick a lot of people have forgotten is that simply posting fresh content on your site automatically moves your site up in the organic search ranks. When you don't keep improving your site with fresh content, you sink in the results because other people are coming in with new stuff. The reason this happens is that new content signals to the search technology that a site has something not seen before by search users. (Want more ideas about improving your ranking in the results? Type "search engine optimization" into one of the reputation aggregators mentioned in this chapter and follow the links to the advice, agencies, and consultants that show up.)

Lost in a Listing of Millions

The importance of search is growing, because we're flooded with information and searchers want answers quickly. Search and the social web are going to be an even more important pairing in the future, because users will want to search, but also want validation from other people. They'll want to hear the opinions and thoughts of other people who've used that product, had that experience, taken that cruise, bought that laptop. Users will want to leave questions for other users or at least read posted comments because these seem more credible than the company's advertising or public relations.

Very simply, you should understand how your customers are using search to find you. You should also explore ways to improve your standing in the results when people search for information about your product, service, issue, or concern.

The Web is so immense—so stuffed with text, audio, video, and growing so rapidly—that it's often difficult to find the exact needle in the virtual haystack. Google, which accounts for about half of all searches, says its mission is "to organize the world's information and make it universally accessible and useful." But as Google itself points out, "there's always more information out there." And it's impossible to tell in a single lifetime whether the Google "laptop" result number

7,294,721 might be the one with the exact information someone has been searching for.

No wonder engineers are always looking for ways to improve search. I'd like to spend the rest of this chapter talking about some of the current activities. I'm listing them in the sure knowledge that by the time you read this there will be more announcements—and it's possible that some of these search engines will have been bought or folded like three of the early search engines, Magellan, AltaVista, and Lycos.

Magellan was a search engine whose popularity plunged after Excite bought it in 1996; Excite killed Magellan when its parent company went bankrupt in 2001. AltaVista says it provides search services and technology and "continues to advance Internet search with new technologies and features designed to improve the search experience for consumers." Lycos now offers entertainment—movies, music, photos, and more; Ask.com provides the site's search function. I see Ask.com as a microcosm of the kind of change that's taking place in search engines.

Don't Ask Jeeves, Just Ask

Ask.com has evolved considerably over the years. It began life as AskJeeves.com, promising users they could use ordinary English to search, for example: "Who has a good value in laptops?" Unfortunately, that didn't work particularly well, and when the dot-com bubble popped, Ask Jeeves almost popped with it. In 2001, however, the company was able to buy Teoma Technologies, and a year later Google made a deal to place ads next to Ask Jeeves search results, which provided a steady cash flow. The company dropped the Jeeves name in early 2006.

Unlike search results that rank results based on the number of links a site has to other websites, the Teoma software first clusters sites based on content categories, then chooses the most popular sites in those categories. That means, says Jim Lanzone, the CEO of Ask.com, his engine does a better job of finding specialized sites that are the most authoritative on a given subject, even though these sites may not be the most popular. "Right now, the focus is almost entirely on improving the user experience," Lanzone told the *New York Times*. "This is the product that, to date, we are the most proud of. It is going to have a huge impact for people who use Ask."

Another innovation is AskCity, a service that integrates maps with information about local businesses, restaurants, concert and movie listings, and reviews. Users who search for a Japanese restaurant in New York City, for instance, will see a listing of the restaurants by neighborhood together with a map pinpointing the locations. Users can search by a specific neighborhood or for another kind of cuisine. Directions are available with a click; users can check out individual restaurant reviews through Citysearch or make reservations through a service called OpenTable, all with a couple of clicks.

Users can also select one restaurant and then search for nearby movies, concerts, or other events, and then book tickets for those events right on the site. AskCity will display walking or driving directions from the restaurant to the movie theater or concert hall. For local marketers—restaurants, movie theaters, entertainment venues— the site can be a good way to reach prospective customers when these people are most interested in a meal and a show.

Because AskCity uses data from sister companies like Citysearch and Ticketmaster, this feature should give Ask a competitive edge since local searches already account for 10 percent of all Internet queries and are expected to grow faster than other searches.

In addition, Ask.com has differentiated itself by giving users previews of the websites that appear in search results and offering simple ways to narrow or expand the results. In a search for the keywords "California and wine," for instance, a set of options will appear next to the results, allowing users to focus their search on, say, California wineries, wine regions, wine prices. It's easy to then expand a query to find Napa wineries, southern California vineyards, or famous foods in California.[7]

Beyond Plain Vanilla Search

What I see coming in reputation aggregators combines scalability of existing search engines with new and improved relevancy models. Search sites are bringing in user preferences, collaboration, collective intelligence, a rich user experience, and other specialized capabilities that make information more *productive*. The following, with no pretense of being comprehensive, is a selection of relatively new approaches to give you a flavor of how the field is changing. Two caveats to keep in mind: The information about these search engines comes mainly from their websites, and I'm not endorsing any one of them. They're here as a service, not as a plug.

EveryZing is an audio and video search engine and online advertising network. Using speech recognition technology, EveryZing searches words within both audio and video, not just the metadata, to classify content based on topic and usage. EveryZing helps consumers find audio and video content based on keyword searches and then allows them to browse the results for relevance, just as text results can be browsed. Consumers can jump to a specific location in the audio and video without fast forwarding or listening to the entire file. On the business side, EveryZing offers marketers online multimedia playback ads tied to consumers' specific search terms and categories. This helps advertisers link directly to the growing volume of video and audio content that consumers go searching for.

Endeca was designed to help people find, analyze, and understand information on individual websites. For example, suppose a consumer visits HomeDepot.com—an Endeca client—and types "drills" in the search box. Search will come back with categories of drills and prices so the user can tailor the search and get more relevant, specific results. This, says Endeca, enables organizations to increase revenue, decrease costs, and streamline operations by helping their customers, employees, and partners find answers to questions quickly and easily. Retailers, manufacturers, distributors, publishers, government agencies, financial services firms, healthcare organizations, hospitality businesses, and professional service providers would find this valuable.

ChoiceStream allows people to personalize the content they receive online, on television, or on a mobile device. No more looking for programs by TV station; instead, users type in "Lost" or some other program name and they can actually watch the program. The search engine becomes the channel aggregator and the television networks just become content providers. Karen Leever, senior vice president,

Directv.com, says: "We chose ChoiceStream because it learns from customer interactions quickly and accurately to understand their unique preferences resulting in a relevant recommendation system that delivers enormous value." For marketers, ChoiceStream is a way to target, connect, and communicate with consumers.

Clusty got its start in Pittsburgh in 2004 when the search software company Vivísimo brought its technology to the Web. But the story really starts in 2000, when Vivísimo was founded by three Carnegie Mellon University scientists tackling the problem of information overload in Web search. Rather than focusing just on search engine result ranking, says cofounder and CEO Raul Valdes-Perez, "we realized that grouping results into topics, or 'clustering,' made for better search and discovery. We're trying to move search away from this idea that ranking Web pages is the solution to everything. Instead, our basic philosophy is, don't just try to show the best ten or the best five pages, but instead dredge up a larger amount of stuff, the top 200 or 500, organize that quickly—in half a second or so, and show the major themes to the user."[8]

Clusty queries several top search engines, combines the results, and generates an ordered list based on comparative ranking. This meta-search approach helps raise the best results to the top but instead of delivering millions of search results in one long list, the search engine groups similar results together into clusters. The clusters not only save users from having to scroll from page to page, they cover results that might have been missed or buried deep in the ranked list. Clusty can also be used to search shopping information, yellow pages data, news, blog posts, and images.

More Flavors of Search

Swicki, like Endeca, is a search tool that an organization can add to its site. Its purpose is to learn and adapt automatically, based on the community's search behavior. Swicki ranks results based on the actions taken by the people who search a site, because there's usually some level of commonality between users of any given site. Swicki's developer,

Eurekster, created it to improve users' search experience, allow websites of all sizes to host search, and enhance search engine marketing for advertisers.

Rollyo and Swicki pursue a similar goal: community powered, theme-based search. Rollyo enables users to create and publish their own personal search engines, based on websites they decide to include in their "Searchroll," Rollyo's name for such a personal engine. With Rollyo, searchers can create personal search engines using only the sources they trust (news articles, blogs, etc.). It requires no programming, and the company offers a starter kit of Searchrolls a user can personalize.

Lexxe, based in Sydney, Australia, has been developing a new generation search engine with advanced natural language processing technologies—similar to the original Ask Jeeves idea. According to the company, "Lexxe has been exploring more intelligent ways to find information for users in a more meaningful way. We believe this method will eventually bring far more accurate and relevant search results than the current search technology."

Wink is a social search engine, searching results that other people have found to be the best results to a particular question. Users re-rank search results, bookmark sites they want to remember, and block results that they don't want to see again. In other words, Wink delivers the results that *users* think are the best. It also lets users create "Collections," gathering the best links for a topic in one place. Users can subscribe to other people's collections, make them public and let other people add to their collections, or make them private so that only the creator can see them.

Gravee is another meta-search engine, which means it combines the results of many different search engines into a single set of results which are further refined by the company's technology. As Gravee users click to "vote" on the relevance of any of the individual results in their searches, the search technology takes those votes into account when displaying future results. Gravee also allows users to add tags (additional keywords describing content) to search results and bookmark their favorite websites with notes and descriptions.

Gravee shares advertising revenue with content owners and compensates them for making search results possible. When a user clicks a keyword search ad on Gravee.com, up to 70 percent of the ad revenue generated is divided between the 10 sites whose content is included in the organic search results on that page. To clarify, that is 70 percent divided by 10, or 7 percent of ad revenue to each website on the organic search results page for every ad clicked.

Jookster is social networking blended with search to help users find content generated by users. More specifically, the site collects photos, videos and bookmarks from sites like YouTube, Flickr, and del.icio.us and puts them in one place for users to search, save, and share with friends.

ZoomInfo offers concise Web summaries with social networking aspects. ZoomInfo, which calls itself a summarization search engine, finds, analyzes, and extracts information from websites, online press releases, electronic news services, and SEC filings. The results are summarized in a comprehensive yet easy-to-read format.

eMvoy is an interesting new entry in business-to-business search. It is for suppliers of plastics and sheet metal, industrial fabrication, machinery and tools, raw materials and chemicals, and services such as testing, assembly, prototyping, and engineering. To make the search results more valuable to the manufacturers who use it, eMvoy rates suppliers on 24 quality, reliability, and stability factors.

All of these should give you a taste of where reputation aggregators are today and where they may go tomorrow. In the future, search will continue further down two paths: contextual and social. Contextual search is where you know the context in which you want to search: My Space, Gather, You Tube, even retail sites like Amazon, Sears, and Ikea.

Social search is where you are asking other people for their experiences: Have you been to St. Kitts? What's your experience with KitchenAid? Can you recommend a good Japanese restaurant in St. Louis? Search is already so important to the social web that you *must* have a strategy for getting into the results for users who matter for you—and for leading new community members to your site.

CHAPTER 13

The Blog Strategy

(Everybody's Talking at Me)

B y the time you read this, the blogosphere will have maxxed out at 100 million blogs. That's right, 100 million blogs—some personal, some professional, all adding their voices to the social web.

From a marketing perspective, a blog can be an excellent tool to build awareness of your company, product, or brand; build trust and strengthen relationships with customers, prospects, employees, and others who are interested or influential; and create a sense of community around the people who are important to your brand's success. So what's your strategy for marketing in the great big blogosphere?

Back in Chapter 10, I suggested sending important bloggers free products or tipping them off to special deals. If this sounds like a no-brainer, pay close attention to the story of Oh! Gizmo (ohgizmo.com). David Ponce is the owner and managing editor of this blog about "gadgets, innovation, and design," where he, senior editor Andrew Liszewski, and their readers blog about the gadgets.

167

In a "Disclosures" section of the site, Ponce clearly states that he and his colleagues are allowed to keep any products sent to them for review purposes. He also emphasizes that they take "great care to maintain our impartiality and will never, for any reason, give a product a positive review when we feel it is undeserved."

Now here's where things get interesting. During an interview, Ponce told a *SmartMoney* magazine writer that a $600 Nokia N91 phone is "great as a music player, but it sucks as an actual phone." In the first Oh! Gizmo review of the product, however, Ponce wrote, "It's solid, powerful and jam-packed with features rarely found all combined in one package like this. Everything works as it should and works well." A follow-up review on Oh! Gizmo softened this opinion: "Things are a little rough around the edges, and turn what would otherwise have been a perfect phone, into, well, one that's slightly less perfect." As *SmartMoney* commented, "Nokia must have been pleased."[1]

I suspect Ponce's comment about the N91 was an unthinking remark he tossed off and was surprised to read in the magazine, but it highlights a couple of key issues. Always be careful what you say to a reporter. And be careful what you say in your blog. The remarks may come back to bite you—once on the Web, they never go away.

So What Is This Thing Called "Blog"?

A blog is a user-generated website on which the writers (bloggers) enter their remarks in journal style, which then appear in reverse chronological order. Blogs often provide commentary or news on a particular subject, such as food, politics, or local news, although some function as more personal online diaries. Like Oh! Gizmo, many blogs also invite readers to comment on the content, including comments about other readers' comments.

A typical blog combines text, images, and links to other blogs, Web pages, and other media related to its topic. The vast majority are primarily text, although some focus on photographs (photo-blog), videos (vlog), or audio (podcasting—more about this later in the chapter), and are part of a wider network of social media.

Blogs aren't anything new. Online diaries and journals began appearing in 1994, and the term *weblog* was coined by Jorn Barger in December 1997. The short form, *blog,* showed up in 1999 and quickly became both a noun and a verb, what the thing is as well as what you do when you're doing it.[2]

Now there are so many blogs that special search tools like Technorati and Google blog search have sprung up. In fact, since Technorati was founded in 2003 by David Sifry, it has tracked the growth of blogs. According to Technorati, the number of blogs doubled about every six months, increasing from fewer than a million in March 2003 to almost 60 million at the end of 2006. Its research shows that every day, more than 100,000 new blogs are created and 1.3 million new posts are added to existing blogs. A few more years of such growth and every man, woman, and child on the planet would have a blog.

However, analysts at Gartner, the technology research company, believe that the number of blogs has leveled out at about 100 million. Why? According to Gartner analyst Daryl Plummer, most of the people who would want to start a blog have already done so. Those who love blogging may be committed to keeping it up while other bloggers become bored and move on. "A lot of people have been in and out of this thing," said Plummer. "Everyone thinks they have something to say until they're put on stage and asked to say it."

As vast as the blogosphere may be, Technorati reports that about 45 percent of the blogs it tracks are not updated more than every three months—if that. And Gartner estimates than more than 200 million people have already stopped writing their blogs.[3]

Communications expert Paul Gillin, of Framingham, Massachusetts, notes that blogging is hardly an American phenomenon. More than a third of all blog posts are in Japanese, and in 2006 Technorati reported the most active blog in the world for a while was Chinese.

Gillin's own survey found that bloggers are active readers:

- 96 percent of the respondents say they regularly read one or more blogs.
- More than 41 percent of respondents read more than 50 blogs a week.
- More than 25 percent read more than 100 blogs a week.

"The message: Bloggers are more likely to read other bloggers," Gillin explains.[4]

Bloggers are also skeptical of marketing. A survey by Edelman public relations focused on how bloggers interact with business. Asked to rate the trustworthiness of various business sources on a 1-to-10 scale, respondents assigned an average value of 4.6 to a message from a public relations firm. Messages that come directly from a company did somewhat better, at 5.5 out of 10.

When Edelman asked, "When looking for product information, which do you trust most?" almost 63 percent of the blogger respondents cited "other bloggers"; only 31 percent noted company websites or press releases. The results confirm the assumption that bloggers are a community bound together by trust. This affinity creates an environment in which one blogger is able to influence many others, leading to vigorous discussion and the occasional swarm.[5]

Blogs Go Big-Time

In the blogosphere, the self-edited and the authoritative tend to rise to the top. Don't make the mistake of assuming that blogs are bloated with half-baked ideas and crackpot opinions. Maybe blogs aren't the *New York Times* or the *Washington Post,* the *New Yorker* or *Reader's Digest,* or even Fox television news. Certainly among the millions of bloggers, a wealth of half-baked crackpots regularly belch their opinions. But readers are quick to point out mistakes. And if the mistakes continue, all but an unreconstructed hard core committed to the source will fall away.

At the same time, I see a new generation of media authority developing rapidly in the blogosphere. I believe the blogosphere is mirroring the evolution of newspapers only in a New York minute. It took decades for the *New York Times, Le Monde,* or the *Financial Times* to become brands, but the Boing Boings and iVillage are becoming trusted information partners to a new generation. They're being held accountable for accuracy by readers rather than by editors and fact-checkers. Blogs will not entirely replace newspapers, but I predict that in five years, no American newspaper will have more than a million (hard copy) readers. Increasingly, consumers and businesspeople will look to blogs for specific, timely, expert information and advice.

Half the news destinations right now are blogs, says Technorati, including the *New York Times,* MSNBC, CNN, the *Washington Post,* the BBC, *USA Today,* NHK, *San Francisco Chronicle* among many others. There is a maturation process in the blogosphere that is going to continue with increased sharing of social media; more and more we'll see "mainstream" media saying, "DailyCandy said . . ." or "Medpundit said . . ." or "WebMD said . . ." or "Boing Boing said . . ." or "The Drudge Report said . . . ."

And, as the blogosphere evolves, bloggers are going to be more professional; they're going to look for more resources. More than a third of the respondents to the Edelman survey said they blog to gain visibility as an authority. (What kind of an authority is often wrong?) In Paul Gillin's survey, one-third of the respondents listed "career advancement" as motivation for blogging, "perhaps reflecting the large number of consultant bloggers." "Overwhelmingly," Gillin says, "people noted intangible factors as being more important, factors like connecting with others, influencing markets, and 'it just feels good.'"

So watch for the blogosphere to become equal to—if not heavier in weight than—traditional media within the next 18 months. With that in mind, how can businesses (large, small, and midsize), employ this tool? Start with the practical issues you confront every day. You can search the blogosphere for the best plastic to use in a certain manufacturing process; or the best distribution network; or the best reseller. Whatever you're looking for, you'll find it discussed and dissected by experts who are blogging.

For example, Doc Searles writes one of the most important blogs for software (doc.weblogs.com/). He's been in the business for three decades, so this is not just somebody who stepped off the bus and says, "I'm going to write a blog about open-source software." This is a man who has studied the subject and can write authoritatively about it. And there are thousands of other experts, specialists in their fields, who like blogging about their ideas and responding to readers' comments.

Get Your People Blogging

The commercial side of the Web is moving from a transactional model—go to a site, buy something, leave—to the social web model—go to a site like a blog, see what people are saying, leave a comment, check out links to other sites, leave a comment, compare user experiences, buy something, comment on the experience, and leave. Josh Scribner, technical project manager and architect in IBM's corporate communications, says that Big Blue is looking hard at this new model.

Josh tells me, "We've been promoting blogs very heavily for the last year and a half. We have some of our executives talking from their own perspective, but at the same time they're talking about topics that are important to the industry. They're talking to investors; they're talking to their business peers; they're talking to CIOs and CTOs and folks like that. This is extremely important because it shows leadership for our brand. Sharing expertise to show leadership is the kind of strategy that any firm can use."

Another Big Blue example comes from Ed Brill, business unit executive, Worldwide Lotus Messaging Sales, IBM Software Group. Brill has been building a community of Lotus software users through his blog (www.edbrill.com) since late 2002. "I found naturally that the people I could get to read the site were my customers, and there was an extended sense of community in my customers. The product we work with is collaborative, and the blog kind of became my way to reach that audience," says Brill. "I found that the one-to-one community interactions became incredibly powerful for decision-making in my own job and for feedback in my own organization. It also keeps me up on competitive trends."[6]

Without a doubt, the best-known corporate blogger is Jonathan Schwartz, the CEO of Sun Microsystems. He says: "My No. 1 priority isn't spending time communicating; it's ensuring that my communications are broadly received. Blogging to me has become the most efficient form of communication. When I blog, I'm talking to the world. I can write a blog in an hour and a half and share something substantive with everyone. But for me to get to Sao Paulo for a meeting with Brazilian customers is easily a two-day operation."

Schwartz notes that about 10 percent of Sun's employees—including the corporate counsel—currently blog, an activity he definitely encourages. "One of the wonderful things about blogs is that I don't have to walk through the campus to figure out what's on people's minds. I just go to blogs.sun.com and I read what they're thinking. It is a daily visit for me."[7]

For Schwartz, blogging reveals the authentic voice of the organization. It is "living the brand." Insincere or phony blogs will not fool anyone for very long—remember the Wal-Mart blunder. Schwartz also believes, as I do, that blogging is an effective and inexpensive way to market the company and its products. "The thing to understand about blogging, and the thing to understand about the Internet as well, is that silence is rarely your friend," says Schwartz. "In a vacuum, somebody else will be speaking on your behalf about your company, about your brands, about your executives or about your employees."

Schwartz told a British reporter he once had an argument with a customer who wanted to know, "Why on earth do you write a blog; it has no impact on me or on the marketplace?" Schwartz's answer: "Well, maybe not on you specifically. But if I'm writing a blog and you're reading it, a journalist is reading, an analyst is reading it, or an investor is reading it—they're not reading something else. They're not reading what my competition has to say. At a certain point, everyone is in competition for your attention. Everyone is in competition for being able to sell you something, being able to appeal to you as a consumer. Advertisers are in competition for your affinity. Employers are in competition for your attention. I want you to pay attention to Sun. The network is a more efficient way of doing that, better than expensive PR."[8]

Think about the internal marketing possibilities that open up when you blog. John Mackey, CEO of Whole Foods Market, recently blogged to explain to employees—and the world—why the company was raising its salary cap. The cap limits the total cash compensation that can be paid to any Whole Foods employee (here called a team ember), from 14 times the average pay to 19 times the average pay. Up to now, a competitive strategy by other supermarkets has been to hire Whole Foods executives.

Here's what Mackey wrote in his blog (available for the world to read at wholefoodsmarket.com/blogs/jm/): "Everyone on the Whole Foods Leadership Team (except for me) has been approached multiple times by 'headhunters' with job offers to leave Whole Foods and go to work for our competitors. Raising the salary cap to 19 times the average pay has become necessary to help ensure the retention of our key leadership."

On his blog, Mackey explained the history of the company's salary cap and noted that the cap doesn't apply to him. "The tremendous success of Whole Foods Market has provided me with far more money than I ever dreamed I'd have and far more than is necessary for either my financial security or personal happiness. I continue to work for Whole Foods not because of the money I can make but because of the pleasure I get from leading such a great company, and the ongoing passion I have to help make the world a better place, which Whole Foods is continuing to do. I am now 53 years old and I have reached a place in my life where I no longer want to work for money, but simply for the joy of the work itself and to better answer the call to service that I feel so clearly in my own heart. Beginning on January 1, 2007, my salary will be reduced to $1 per year and I will no longer take any other cash compensation at all."[9]

I noticed that Mackey's blog entry was followed by comments and questions about the new policy, both congratulating the company for leading by example and skeptical. For example, "Shareholders (many of them team members) are getting crushed today . . . absolutely crushed. I wonder what type of negative impact this will have on morale and retention going forward." Maybe employees or shareholders would have made these kinds of comments in a survey or annual meeting, but maybe not. I think Mackey's blog was the right place for give-and-take discussion.

You Do Want to Hear the Bad News

But isn't there a danger in allowing just anybody inside and outside the company to say anything in public? What about competitive information? Trade secrets? Proprietary data? After all, loose lips sink ships.

Yes, there's a danger. So for comments coming from outside the company, I agree that it's both legitimate and prudent to screen out the irrelevancies, obscenities, and liabilities. The Whole Foods site warns readers: "Only comments specifically addressing issues discussed in John Mackey's blog post will be posted. . . . Business propositions sent to this blog will not be reviewed."

Every responsible senior executive wants to hear the bad news, whether it's a negative reaction to a new policy or a customer gripe that could be an early sign of something far worse. The problem, says Jonathan Schwartz, is the natural tendency to keep bad news away from the boss. He says that Scott McNealy, Sun's chairman and former CEO, told him, "Always worry about what people aren't telling you."

That said, however, you can't have it both ways. You can't invite outsiders to comment on company products, policies, and performance and allow only the enthusiastic or innocuous to be heard. These days, word will get out faster than you can imagine, and the firm's timidity will be exposed. I believe it's far better to take your lumps and correct the problem. As Josh Scribner at IBM says, you want to head off problems or be able to address them. "IBM has been making a great effort to keep an eye on what's going on out there and listen to what our customers have to say."

What about bloggers within the company? How can you confidently allow employees to blog?

When I have this discussion with senior executives, I can only respond with question: Do you trust your employees? Do they cheat on their expense accounts? Steal company supplies? Freelance during company hours? If there's no trust between employees and managers, if managers believe that most employees are basically dishonest and looking for a way to rip off the organization, then allowing employees to blog about the company is probably a bad idea. (Obviously, the company cannot stop an employee from blogging about, say, her gardening challenges, when she's at her home computer and on her own time.)

If, however, senior management believes that most employees are basically honest, the issue is one of guidelines rather than control. Josh says that when IBM decided to go into blogs in a big way, management carefully considered the issues and established guidelines for employee bloggers. These guidelines included "things like: don't get into an argument with people, because there's no point. Be the first to apologize. Say who you are. We want people to say who they are and to say that their opinions are not necessarily those of IBM."

Still, Josh knows that companies worry about what might happen if an employee blogger says something wrong or inflammatory or otherwise inappropriate. What then? "You need to make sure that it is clearly explained that they are talking on their own behalf, because that will satisfy a company's legal team. That's how we work with our own legal team here."

IBM also insists on transparency, meaning employees must say they work for IBM if they blog about IBM. This is critical, Josh emphasizes, because readers should "feel we're being honest when we're out there. We don't have subterfuge in the blogging world."

Rules for Employees Who Blog

Let me go back to Sun for a moment because it's so active in encouraging employees to blog. Browsing the "About Sun" section of its website, I found that the company posts employee blogging guidelines with this introduction: "Many of us at Sun are doing work that could change the world. We need to do a better job of telling the world. As of now, you are encouraged to tell the world about your work, without asking permission first (but please do read and follow the advice in this note)." Because these guidelines are so apt and well-written, I want to include some here (picked up almost verbatim from Sun's site):

- *It's a two-way street.* The real goal isn't to get everyone at the company blogging, it's to become part of the industry conversation. . . . If you start writing, remember the Web is all about links; when you see something interesting and relevant, link to it; you'll be doing your readers a service, and you'll also generate links back to you; a win-win.

- *Don't tell secrets.* Common sense at work here; it's perfectly okay to talk about your work and have a dialog with the community, but it's not okay to publish the recipe for one of our secret sauces.

- *Be interesting.* Writing is hard work. There's no point doing it if people don't read it. Fortunately, if you're writing about a product that a lot of people are using, or are waiting for, and you know what you're talking about, you're probably going to be interesting. And because of the magic of hyperlinking and the Web, if you're interesting, you're going to be popular, at least among the people who understand your specialty.

    Another way to be interesting is to expose your personality; almost all of the successful bloggers write about themselves, about families or movies or books or games; or they post pictures. People like to know what kind of a person is writing what they're reading. Once again, balance is called for; a blog is a public place and you should try to avoid embarrassing your readers or the company.

- *Write what you know.* The best way to be interesting, stay out of trouble, and have fun is to write about what you know.

- *Financial rules.* There are all sorts of laws about what we can and can't say, business-wise. Talking about revenue, future product ship dates, road maps, or our share price is apt to get you, or the company, or both, into legal trouble.

- *Quality matters.* Use a spell-checker. If you're not design oriented, ask someone who is whether your blog looks decent, and take his or her advice on how to improve it. You don't have to be a great or even a good writer to succeed at this, but you do have to make an effort to be clear, complete, and concise. Of course, "complete" and "concise" are to some degree in conflict; that's just the way life is. There are very few first drafts that can't be shortened, and usually improved in the process.

- *Think about consequences.* The worst thing that can happen is that one of our sales reps is in a meeting with a hot prospect, and someone on the customer's side pulls out a print-out of your blog and says "This person at your company says that product sucks." In general, "XXX sucks" is not only risky but unsubtle. Once again, it's all about judgment: Using your blog to trash or embarrass the company, our customers, or your coworkers, is not only dangerous but stupid.[10]

Diving into the Blogosphere

"I can't even imagine how Jonathan Schwartz has the time to write what he does write," says Halley Suitt, a former CEO and an active blogger.[11] She's been blogging since 2002, encouraged by her friend David Weinberger, one of the authors of *The Cluetrain Manifesto*. It's so fast and easy to write and publish in the blogosphere, she explains, and it allows you to have a discussion with readers in context.

"Two years after I started blogging," Halley tells me, "I tried to write a letter to someone instead of an e-mail, and I found I kept writing in HTTP: I was actually writing in links. My life had become so connected to the Web that I couldn't even write a plain, hey-how-are-you-doing letter without mentioning 10 links. I finally threw the letter away and sent an e-mail, because it had links to things I'm doing and care about and want them to read."

As a long-time blogger who has spoken about blogs at conferences, Halley has some good ideas for company bloggers. First, blog often. The posts can be short—indeed, shorter is usually better—and they should be entertaining. Your blog should be connected to and engaged with the blogging community in your arena. Get to know the other people who write on your subject and engage with them. In her words, "A poor blog is a lackluster blog with one perfectly polished blog post a week that looks like overkneaded pastry. Deadly. A poor blog sounds like the public relations department wrote it two weeks ago and 30 executives approved it—who cares?"

Should CEOs blog? Halley can go both ways on this. "I have good reasons why they should not blog, and also good reasons why they should. If the CEO is a good writer and wants to be part of the conversation on the blogosphere—if it won't be the PR person writing the blog—I say go ahead and do it." Still, she suspects very few CEOs qualify as enthusiastic, easy writers. Most CEOs are too busy and are privy to confidential things that shouldn't be mentioned in a blog.

In addition, blogging takes an enormous amount of commitment and dedication, Halley says: "If you're a blogger, you need to know the other players in the blogosphere, you should be reading other blogs and posting comments on them. Blogging is more like a quilting bee than knitting your own sweater. There's a patchwork community of blogs across the whole blogosphere, with each blogger working on one small square while reacting to the other bloggers and what they care about. You only blog well if you're serious about engaging with the blogging community."

In other words, you have to make time to read blogs related to your field, understand who's blogging and why, and actively participate in the conversation. Halley practices what she preaches: "Every morning when I get up, I look at blogs to see who is writing about what and decide whether I want to jump in and comment on the subject of the day. If you want to commit to that extent, then do it. But know that there is the commitment." Influencing other blogs ought to be part of your marketing strategy. If you want to be part of the blogosphere, if you want people to share their comments on your site, you have to go share on theirs.

Executives should also think carefully about what might happen if they provoke the community and how they might want to respond in such a situation. Moreover, she says, be ready to respond promptly. If you travel frequently and can't check your blog on a regular basis, you might not want to blog at all.

If your CEO isn't about to give his life over to a blog, Halley suggests starting a group company blog using managers or employees throughout the organization, which has the added bonus of giving readers a sense of all the different teams under one roof. Occasional blog posts from members of the executive team are great, so don't set the expectation that the blog is only written by one person all the time, much less the CEO. The exception to this rule is a CEO who really wants to be the voice of the company, really knows how to write and *really* understands the time commitment that blogging requires.

The CEO can write occasionally, when the situation demands it (as when Whole Foods changed its salary cap, for example, and Mackey blogged an explanation). But so could people from the manufacturing group, from sales and marketing, from finance, from human resources, from every function. Says Halley, "I would want a diversity of voices throughout my company."

You can either make your group company blog public and available to outsiders for comment or keep it private, strictly for internal bloggers and readers. That's a major decision and, Halley adds, "the most undiscovered area of blogging—internal blogging. I think it's really valuable to have internal blogs where people are blogging to each other and sharing expertise. You don't have to have a public blog. A CEO may choose to have internal blogs that are very useful to the people inside and avoid airing issues that shouldn't be discussed in public."

One last thought on blogging: If something happens in your business at 11:12 A.M., you can blog about it at 11:13 A.M. If someone disses you or says your company has committed an error, a crime, or a bad deed, you can react instantly. That's the beauty of blogging.

Marketers should also be aware that advertising will be coming soon to the blogosphere. A number of software companies are developing programs that eventually will permit a marketer to post ads within the posts. They'll be very topical and focused. If someone writes a blog on plastics and you're a plastics manufacturer, that's the place for you.

Of course, you want to know that someone is reading the blog. In fact, before you buy an ad, you'll want to know as much as possible about the blog's audience. Who it reaches, where they live, demographics, psychographics, behavior, and more. That hasn't been done in the blogosphere yet—or hadn't when I wrote this paragraph—and I think it's because there isn't a lot of advertising. But I encourage marketers to do a deep dive to analyze the top tier blogs, the ones most important to their communities.

Now Listen Up! Podcasting Is Here

I don't want to close this chapter without a few words about podcasting.

A podcast is a media file that creators—companies or individuals—distribute by subscription (paid or unpaid) over the Internet using syndication feeds, for playback on mobile devices and personal computers. Though podcasters' websites may offer direct download or streaming of their content, a podcast is distinguished from other digital audio formats because you can download it automatically using software capable of reading feed formats.

Podcasting's technical components were available by 2001 and started showing up on well-known websites in 2003. A bit of trivia: Podcasting was named the word of the year by the editors of the *New Oxford American Dictionary* in 2005. The word provoked some controversy because it seems to imply that an Apple iPod is needed to listen to podcasts, when in fact all portable media players (and most newer PCs and laptops) will play them.

Initially, podcasting's appeal was that individuals could distribute their own "radio shows." It didn't take long for the system to be adapted to a wide variety of other uses, including distribution of school lessons, official and unofficial audio tours of museums, conference meeting alerts and updates, and public safety messages.

Podcasting is an increasingly popular communication tool for staying in touch with customers and other important audiences. Sun Microsystems offers at least a dozen podcasts on its website, including a "news" podcast about the latest from Sun and interviews with various Sun engineers and executives. One recent podcast featured the Sun CEO and an expert on sustainable development discussing "how the Internet and technology can enable communities and environmental solutions."

Then there's Sun's Virtually Everywhere Podcast, which "allows you to listen to Sun innovators, customers, and partners discuss your top IT and business pain points and find out how Sun software and solutions can help you solve them."[12] Think how valuable it would be to have your customers talking about their problems and then listening to how your company can solve these "pain points." That's the power of podcasting.

And the use continues to spread. Unilever recently announced that it would sponsor "The Masthead with Marie Claire." Joanna Coles, *Marie Claire*'s editor, was the host of five-minute podcasts that provided an inside look at the making of the magazine. *Marie Claire* promoted the episodes on marieclaire.com, msn.com, and podshow.com. And Unilever, as sponsor, was able to reinforce its brand and positioning with a key target audience.

You can't afford to sit back while competitors jump on the podcasting or blogging bandwagon. If you want to be seen as a market leader, if you want to reinforce your ties to customers, if you want to shape the conversation, go out and make a place for yourself on the social web right now.

CHAPTER 14

The E-Community Strategy

(Go to Their Party or Throw Your Own)

If the blogosphere holds hundreds of millions of blogs, the Web has hundreds of thousands of e-communities. Back in Chapter 7, in the discussion of building your own community, I defined e-communities as sites where people aggregate around professionally generated content focused on a common interest area. Whether the common interest is business or personal, people join these communities and return to them regularly because they offer news, information, entertainment, or all three, content primarily generated by professionals. In this chapter, I want to talk about how you can connect with somebody else's e-community or build your own e-community to reach the people who matter to your business.

Thousands of e-communities are already drawing sizable audiences, with new sites being established daily. The pioneer—and prototypical—e-community was Slate, which Microsoft founded in 1966. Michael Kinsley, Slate's founding editor, says that for the first few years it was referred to as "Slate, Microsoft's experimental online magazine that some people read on their computer via the Internet." Today they say, "Slate reported yesterday." By my definition, Slate has a number of e-communities: news and politics, arts and life, business and technology, health and science, style and shopping, travel and food, and sports. These are communities not only because of the common interests that members share, but because Slate's visitors can comment on and discuss the articles posted by the professional writers and reporters.

In an interview on Slate's 10th anniversary, Kinsley said he was proudest of the fact that the site breaks even, "at least part of the time. I said from the beginning, the test would be if it was self-supporting. And even though the experiment with charging for subscriptions didn't work out, the idea that the Washington Post Company paid serious money for it makes me very happy." On the other hand, "One thing we never mastered was long-form journalism on the Web. Articles that might appear in the *New Yorker* or the *Atlantic*. Of course, no one else has figured out how to do it, either."[1]

Let me use Slate to make two key points: First, Web content has to be extraordinarily valuable for subscribers to pay anything for it. And second, few people want to read long documents on their computer screen. (That could change. If handheld electronic readers become popular, people may be willing to download long articles as well as books.)

Babble for a New Generation

If Slate is one of the first e-communities, Babble.com is one of the latest. At the end of 2006, Nerve Media introduced what it called "the first parenting magazine designed from the ground up for a new generation of parents—mothers and fathers who increasingly share the work of raising children, live in cities, and use the Internet to access information."

Babble will have to work to build its community. As the *New York Times* pointed out, newsstands and library archives are filled with current and departed parenting magazines, and today's Web is full of mommy and daddy blogs, message boards like UrbanBaby.com and social networking sites like Maya's Mom (mayasmom.com, "where parents share") and MothersClick.com ("Connecting. Learning. Sharing").

At the same time, Babble is looking at a big market. According to 2004 Census data, 78 percent of women ages 30 to 44 are mothers. Also men, a big target readership of Babble, are more attentive to their children than previous generations. A University of Maryland study, "Changing Rhythms of American Family Life," found that married fathers spent 6.5 hours a week on child care in 2000, up from 2.6 hours in 1965.

Julia Beck, founder of 40 Weeks, a consultancy serving the expectant- and new-parent market, said, "This is a new generation of parents who are interested in taking their existing lifestyle, sense of self and priorities into parenting, as opposed to checking them at the parenthood door. They're looking for ways to infuse their personality and aesthetic into this new phase of life, and all this new lifestyle parenting media reflects that."[2]

Because it's very unlikely that Babble will be able to sell subscriptions (actually, there's no indication that it will even try), the site will have to do what magazine publishers have long had to do: attract an audience—or an e-community—that the publication can sell to advertisers who want to reach it. Like any medium, it will have to convince media buyers that it actually has an audience and that the audience has characteristics important to the advertiser. That's where you get your opportunity to go to somebody else's party, mingle with visitors, and maybe invite them to a party of your own.

Electrons Beat Paper and Ink

An online e-community like Babble or Slate has a number of advantages for both publishers and readers that a paper-and-ink publication does not have, however, including:

- It pays nothing for printing, binding, and postage. (It does pay for bandwidth, but generally nowhere near as much.)
- The site contains moving images and sound as well as text and color photos.
- Information can be timely; there's no gap between writing a story and publishing it. (Michael Kinsley says the idea that anything could be posted instantaneously didn't occur to Slate's staff at first. They learned quickly; "I'd be writing a column and send it in and then go out for a sandwich and if it wasn't up when I got back, I'd bitch about it.")
- An online publication can link to other sites on the Web; one click and a reader jumps to a source, a company report, or something else that adds to the article's depth and richness.
- An online publication accumulates an archive of material that community members can search; nothing ever goes out of print.
- Such a publication has virtually unlimited space for reader comment.
- Given the nature of the Internet, the publisher can measure reader interest and advertising response in a depth and detail that's not practical for a paper-and-ink publication.

What's in It for You?

E-communities—online parties hosted by Slate and others—can be excellent places for companies to advertise and participate in the discussions. A potential advertiser, for example, can check out Slate's brief online media kit: "Over 5 million people visit Slate each month . . . 64 percent are college graduates . . . 44 percent have an annual household income of $75,000 . . . 96 percent have shopped online for products or services . . . 20 percent have shopped online for investment purposes . . . 40 percent hold a professional or managerial position . . . 30 percent have shopped online for business-to-business products/services" and more.

I suspect Slate's salespeople have the same challenge selling advertising as general-interest publications like the *Washington Post, New York
Times, Time, Newsweek, Reader's Digest,* and the *New Yorker.* It's somewhat easier to sell ads on, say, a parenting site where the readers' interests are more naturally aligned with the marketer's products. Gerber,
Fisher-Price, Pampers, Kid Cuisine, and many other marketers want to
go to the parenting party and can add some value for visitors, as well.

It's important to distinguish e-communities from, say, the communities of MySpace or YouTube. E-communities largely contain professional
content with a leaven of reader comment, whereas the other communities mix user-generated with some professional content. My view is there
will be a continual mix for the next few years. High-end professional
content will continue to reign in e-communities such as the *New England Journal of Medicine,* WebMD, Sermo.com, SmartMoney,
ESPN.com, and others. Increasingly we'll see a mix of user-generated
content and professional. Examples of that might be Gather.com,
Tickle.com, or Expedia.com, which is more like a social network.

E-communities are going to be an increasingly important digital-
only category for connecting with and maintaining some kind of relationship with your most valued customer groups. Now this is where
paid advertising can really pay off on the Web. I see advertising becoming more diffused: not all the money will be going into reaching
the vast television audience—instead, marketers will be spending to
reach highly targeted audiences, putting much smaller amounts of
money into advertising about, say, bass fishing in northern Idaho or
bass fishing in Mississippi.

Start thinking this way and all sorts of opportunities open up
when you look for e-communities. Suppose a car enthusiast subscribes
to *Motor Trend* (or *Car and Driver*). On motortrend.com, he can read
blogs about the latest Motown news, car designs, concept cars, and
more; subscribe to the magazine's e-newsletter and add his two cents
to several discussion forums. From videos of the magazine's road tests
to virtual road tests and simulations, this car guy will feel like he's at
the wheel on the open road, at the track, or wherever.

Still on motortrend.com, he can download both of the magazine's
weekly podcasts; see the magazine's video coverage of the latest car

shows; check out behind the scenes videos of special car events and car-related entertainment; cast his vote in online polls; enter a subscription to the print version of the magazine. And he can compare and price new and used vehicles with just a couple of clicks (and look for car insurance at the same time). Nearly all of this is professional content that covers the vast spectrum of car enthusiasts' interests. And those are just the links from one of the many car-related sites. Various ads for car-related goods and services share the screen with much of the content I've outlined here (as on caranddriver.com, as another example).

Marketers should be aware of the opportunities that tie communities together or cut across communities. So cars lead naturally to communities about cars (or trucks or SUVs) and racing (NASCAR, Formula One, whatever), cars and in-dash entertainment centers, cars and tricked-out accessories, cars and tires, cars and driving, cars and insurance, cars and luggage carriers, cars and ski racks, cars and bicycle racks, antique cars and trucks, car shows, car clubs, car movies, cars and travel, cars and repair services.

Marketers have to be at the intersections where interest areas connect with other topics. Because if you're not at those intersections in the e-community, someone else is going to be there. If Goodrich Tires wasn't advertising on caranddriver.com, then Michelin should be. Same for auto insurance and all the other intersections that make sense for the car enthusiast e-community.

Throw Your Own Party

For years we've been on this drug of mass media, thinking that the more money we invest in television spots, the more we'll sell. I just don't see it. Madison Avenue will continue to fight for television spots, arguing that the numbers are there. But even though viewership is off the charts for the Super Bowl, does that mean ads during the Super Bowl sell that much more beer . . . or cars . . . or salty snacks? Here's an alternative.

Instead of spending all your advertising money on a fun beer ad, why not divert some to the Web? If you're Coors, you can create an e-community that focuses on hiking trips in the Rockies, white water rafting in Colorado . . . best films made of the Rocky Mountains. Start building a community, don't just try to sell beer. Get away from the idea that you have to use television, radio, and print ads to tell people to just buy, buy, buy. Tell them more about the environment you love. People will come to your special e-community even if they happen to drink Heineken right now, because Heineken is not offering promotions to go white water rafting in the Rockies, tours in the Rockies, bed and breakfasts in Aspen, and so on. Now you've got a number of marketers coming to *your* party and bringing their professional content to intrigue your community's members.

I believe that this is where marketing is going. Draw millions of people to an e-community and many marketers will want to come to that party. If it's your party, you can charge for advertising space or take a small commission for every sale made by one of your online partners. If it's not your party, you can arrange to be invited and join the discussion with blogs or forums or other content. The cross connections are there for you to explore.

E-Communities Expand the World

The significance of the e-community for the car enthusiast or the DIYer or the skier or anybody is that it's incredibly easy to make these connections, hear other people's opinions, participate, and share. Before, you might have heard about a car show because you read about it in the local paper or you were on somebody's mailing list. But nondigital communication was a lot less efficient and a lot less appealing in some ways (and certainly a lot more hit or miss).

The time is coming when we will share our interests with people for certain periods. Take my car enthusiast example. He—or she—will be able to say, "For the next hour I am going to entertain offers. You know I'm interested in cars or trucks or vans, you know generally how much I spend and what I like. Make me an offer." Rather than the current situation where airlines and hotel chains are offering last-minute, weekend deals, the consumer consciously decides when he or she is ready to entertain business offers.

If I were a marketer in the pharmaceutical/life sciences industries, I'd want to ensure a presence in the most topical e-communities that draw millions of people, such as WebMD's different communities. How do I get my firm included in the chats and the presentations, articles, white papers, and the podcasts? If I were Pfizer, I'd want the senior medical executive for high cholesterol drugs on a podcast talking about the latest advancements in those drugs. The idea is to develop programs and campaigns for getting your company's name, content, and information into the e-communities where your target audiences regularly go.

In the past, you might have felt your company had to be in a relevant magazine, or on a television news show, or on the newspaper's health page. Now you want to participate in the appropriate e-community. Even if you can't actually get onto the site except through paid advertising, you certainly can be linked in its stories. How about cooperating via your site? For car enthusiasts, BMW can offer blogs, videos, podcasts, interviews, sneak peeks, and much more.

In the computer industry, Hewlett Packard has a good example of doing just this. HP engaged John Gallant, the editorial director of *Network World* magazine, to conduct interviews with CEOs and CIOs about tech topics like the future of the datacenter. These interview podcasts are posted for download on the HP site. In other words, HP is bringing an outside professional to help generate new, interesting content that's directly relevant to its e-community.

Add Your Voice

Another way to use e-communities is through the chat rooms. Become familiar with the various e-community chat rooms where your customers go, so you can try to interest some of those audiences in coming to your party. If people are regularly logging on to WebMD and spending time there, how can Genzyme attract them to its party? Try sharing information in the chat areas, or the bulletin boards, or posting questions. Or participate in the e-community's blog to raise awareness of your company and what it's doing. If somebody is commenting on the WebMD site or any other site and there's a place for comment, you can comment as well. You can comment on the comments. The thread keeps going, and, on the Web, it exists forever. Make yourself part of the e-community conversation.

Previously, the only way you could interact with a magazine if you were an everyday Joe was send a letter to the editor and hope it got printed. In an e-community, the everyday Joes and the marketing professionals both have far more potential for a far more influential voice in what is going on.

Of course, certain e-communities are quasi-professional. As I said many chapters ago, the line between these categories is not solid. Some e-communities border on a combination of blogs and professional content. In your Observe phase, therefore, you have to identify not only the significant bloggers but also the growing e-communities of professional content that can influence audiences important to your marketing efforts.

Look at their content. What are they trying to do? Most of them will tell you. What can you add? Most editors are hungry for new information, new leads, new voices. All successful companies have experts and thought leaders whose ideas and observations would be of interest to the editors and the writers of the e-communities.

E-communities will become the preferred resource for today's generation the way magazines were for an older generation. The parents of yesterday had *Parents*, the parents of today have Babble.com. (Actually, the new generation has Babble.com *and* Parents.com. Significantly, Parents.com opened with a subscription offer for the paper-and-ink magazine, three years for $9. That $9 would not cover three years of postage.) The older generation had *Forbes*, the new generation has Forbes.com. The big difference is that in the older world, magazines, newspapers, radio, and television were one-way communication. In the e-communities, members take only what they want, take as much as they want, and talk back. One more time: *Marketing is a dialogue.*

CHAPTER

15

The Social
Networks Strategy

(Connecting with a Click)

T
alk about a level playing field: marketing to social networks is
a viable strategy for businesses large and small. Here's how
one midsize company (with $44 million in annual sales) is
using a social network to market its products under the screen name
of MerlynDHZ.

MerlynDHZ has posted a bunch of homemade videos of young
men doing really cool tricks in their Heelys—sneakers with retractable
wheels in the soles—on the YouTube social network site. (You can
find one of these videos by searching for "Heelys General Teaser
Video.") Viewers can watch the kids fly down and up a halfpipe, zip
along a railing, and more. MerlynDHZ not only posts the videos, but
also answers questions from viewers who sometimes have shaky

spelling: "Damn, do you practice a lot? I just recentley got my heelys and i'm just getting used to turning lol, BTW, where do you get the grinding heelys?"

MerlynDHZ is actually David Chau, who works for Heeling Sports Limited, the Carrollton, Texas, company that makes Heelys. Like Burger King, Smirnoff, and others, Heeling Sports posts short videos to generate buzz via social networks. Brooks Radighieri, the company's marketing manager, told *Inc. Magazine* that the homemade quality of the clips appeals to the firm's target market, kids who are constantly battered by ads. "It has more validity if it doesn't look like a corporate-sponsored video," she said. "Kids are sharp—they know when you're trying to sell them something."[1]

It's a vid, vid, vid, vid world: "Videos seem to have replaced the jokes in my in-box," says Stefan Tornquist, research director at MarketingSherpa, a Rhode Island research firm. In fact, the Online Publishers Association reports that 7 out of 10 Internet users have watched an online video, and 30 percent of those people have shared one with friends, usually via e-mail. The same study found that viral videos translate into sales. Sixty-six percent of the people who watch videos online have seen an ad clip; about one-third of those viewers visited the marketer's website; and 8 percent have made a purchase.[2] As Reid Hoffman at LinkedIn noted, bringing video contact online is similar to the print to television revolution. "Sudden this is a much more emotionally and socially engaging medium. There is much more social interaction for me to be watching someone's own little music video than to be reading a long blog post."

Radighieri at Heeling Sports admits that his company's YouTube campaign hasn't had the same effect on sales as, say, the company's commercials on Nickelodeon. Still, she's happy with the low-cost exposure. "It's helping us build brand recognition," she says. With the social networks strategy, you too can build or reinforce brand recognition, connect with your targeted audiences, and leverage your marketing messages.

Everything Old Is New Again

By now you know that social networks are member-based online communities that enable users to link to one another based on common interests. Unlike e-communities, they have mainly user-generated content rather than material produced by professionals or experts. In addition to YouTube, well-known examples include MySpace, FaceBook, Friendster, Eons, Flikr, and more. (Wikipedia lists more than 80 "social networking sites.")

Nonvirtual social networks have been around for centuries. From the Industrial Revolution until fairly recently, much of life outside of work involved people in social networks like the church, the lodge, the Lions, Elk, Moose, Odd Fellows, Masons, bowling leagues, sewing circles, bridge clubs, political clubs, and much, much more. Networks with a professional angle—such as Rotary, Kiwanis, and thousands of industry-specific organizations—are all "social networks" in their nature. Also, what's been the most popular place on a college campus throughout the past hundred years? (Hint: Not the library.) Probably the student union, although fraternities and sororities are also forms of social networks.

While such social networks never went away, they certainly declined after World War II. As Harvard sociologist Robert Putnam wrote in his seminal 1995 book *Bowling Alone:* "Television, two-career families, suburban sprawl, generational changes in values—these and other changes in American society have meant that fewer and fewer of us find that the League of Women Voters, or the United Way, or the Shriners, or the monthly bridge club, or even a Sunday picnic with friends fits the way we have come to live."[3]

The extraordinary growth of social networks on the Web suggests that many people recognize a human need for such connections and are trying to find them as best they can. The technology industry, especially the software industry, which is only about 30 years old, started "user groups" early on. A company like Lotus or Microsoft or Oracle would pay to bring its software users together to enjoy speakers and educational content, refreshments, and entertainment as a way to

spread the word about the software. After a few years, company sponsorship dropped off as users started paying their own way because they
wanted to spend time with other users, giving and getting the latest
tips and tricks.

Even as we had become desocialized for all the reasons Putman
identified, when we were spending more time alone and developing a
more focused interests in specific topics like games, sex, medicine,
sports, and more, there was a breakthrough in the digital realm.
Given the human drive for community, it makes sense that we would
evolve and create some kind of digital social atmosphere.

Click and Connect

The first online social networks really began in 1999 with a company
called Emode, founded by James Currier. Emode (which changed its
name to Tickle) was a pioneer in getting people to fill out question-
naires online. What is your interest? What do you like to do? The
software would then match people within a community based on similar interests. That was a surprisingly brave new idea way back when.
Tickle was eventually bought by Monster.com and today offers members more than 200 personality, career, and entertainment tests,
promising to deliver "a deep, rich, and meaningful way for people to
connect with one another."

For marketers, Tickle offers a convenient way to reach out to a
self-selected group of prospective customers and understand their
demographic, personality, career, and behavioral characteristics.
Not long ago, Procter & Gamble's Cover Girl brand turned to
Tickle to reach teen girls and young women, extend its seasonal
"color" promotions online, and build a database. Tickle developed a
series of seasonal themed beauty quizzes relevant to Cover Girl's
products and embedded an opt-in question in the quizzes to build
the database. The results (at least the ones that P&G will reveal): 5
percent of the young women who took the quizzes clicked through
to Cover Girl, and opt-ins averaged over 2,000 a week during the
promotion.

In many ways, Amazon was an early social network. Although it had a specific commercial goal—to sell lots of books—the architecture was one of community. The idea was that you got to know the site, the people, the things that were happening, what people were saying, what was available to buy, and join the conversation. Amazon wasn't (isn't) just an online retailer selling you books, it was soliciting your opinion about the books (and, now, everything else it sells).

Then Friendster went live in 2003, and because it was ready-made for uploaded images, the burgeoning digital camera craze made Friendster more successful than the older Six Degrees (which managed to attract about 10 million people but could not get them to come back). Social networks are increasingly popular for personal and professional use. Now, says Reid Hoffman, the founder of the social network LinkedIn, "you have the ability to browse your social network and find out interesting things about who people really are. Some of that is about dating, about 'Is the person cute?' But also some of it is about making the whole thing much more human."

The wired world is taking full advantage of, well, how our brains are wired to recognize and respond to faces and interpersonal interaction. "Suddenly this is a much more emotionally and socially engaging medium from the viewpoint of tying to the emotional infrastructure," says Reed. "In fact, people like looking at people. It's much more social interaction for me to be watching people creating their own little music videos than to be reading a long blog post."

And the technology means that people can take and swap both still and moving images from their digital cameras, video cameras, cell phones, and laptops. As the technology improves, the pictures will improve and the whole social network experience will become that much richer. Already, for many people, participation in one or more social networks is taking the place of watching television or reading a book or a magazine.

I don't think peoples' nature has changed that much; despite our busy, modern lifestyles, we are still social beings. The venue today is more digital than the Grange Hall or the church basement. If you buy my argument that human beings really want to belong to specific types of social networks, and if you also buy my argument that the

Web is increasingly the next-closest thing to physical life without actually being in another person's presence, you understand the phenomenal growth of online social networks.

Facebook clearly tapped into a real interest and desire to connect, something that kids readily responded to. It was founded at Harvard in 2004 and just three years later had almost eight million members, fueled by word of mouse. Remember, if marketing is about aggregating, how much do you think Facebook spent on advertising? Not a thing. Neither did MySpace (120 million members) or YouTube (20 million visitors a month). Their meteoric growth alone tells us something about what they're tapping into.

This changing face of social networks really means that people like to belong to certain communities. They like the information and they like the people even though they are not physically meeting them. Not everyone, of course. I've heard people of a certain age say, "Talking to a stranger online sounds really scary." Well, yes, it can be. But how many times have you waited for a bus or been in an elevator or stood in a supermarket line and carried on a five-minute conversation with a stranger? Maybe something connected, or maybe you had nothing in common and that was the end of the connection. But technology has the ability to capture patterns in people's behaviors and connect you to other people with similar interests and backgrounds. Think of Amazon's ability, based on your buying behavior, to suggest books in which you might be interested or Netflix's ability to suggest movie titles.

Social network sites include wine clubs, sports clubs, recipe exchanges, so it is not just MySpace, Facebook, and YouTube. If I were head of marketing at Gallo or Beringer or Kendall Jackson, I would want to be in front of people in the wine clubs, alerting them to this week's tasting sessions in, say, Albany, Indianapolis, and Oklahoma City. I would like to let them know there are discounts on my cases in these 37 states. But don't ever forget that the community controls the club itself. The community decides whether there will be commercial messages, based on the site's need for revenue and service to the members.

To influence these communities, I believe, companies should do something for the social good—donate a playground; donate to breast cancer research; donate lumber to Habitat for Humanity. Even better, be sure that you and others in your organization get personally involved by volunteering your time and talents to whatever it is that will make you and your community prouder, stronger, healthier, happier. (One of my pet projects, for example, is the $150 laptop to bridge the digital divide.)

Focus on Focused Social Networks

The next generation of consumer social networks will have much smaller, far more focused networks—which helps the midsize and small marketer as well as the biggest enterprises. Pick some sort of very specific interest related to your product or service, be it model trains, home brewing, or scrapbooking; find the social networks in that arena; and see how you can participate.

The social network strategy is not just for consumer goods marketing; it's also profoundly useful for business-to-business marketing. Dentists, doctors, butchers, bakers, and candlestick makers all may have an interest in social networks. Right now, LinkedIn and Monster are perhaps the best-known business-to-business social networks. However, if you're a large enterprise, you can start creating an online destination around what you do, your products, and your technology, tapping into the interests of your customer base. (Pick up a highlighter and look back at the chapters in Part II for a start.)

As an example, think about the narrow focus of Genzyme, which works to discover successful drug therapies for rare diseases. If my child had a rare disease, I would want to know about the Genzyme community. I'd want to know why it costs so much to develop a drug for my child's disease. I'd want to meet other parents with children suffering from the same illness. For Genzyme to facilitate those contacts and bring me that information would be much more powerful for Genzyme than if I were to obtain it somewhere else, say from Google or from raredisease.org.

The opportunity here is to show that you're an important community source for authentic information, not just marketing hype. In the business-to-business world, IBM has been a business machine and computing technology company longer than anybody on the planet and has more patents in its fields than anybody else. So if you're a technology/software buyer, you would reason that IBM must have something thoughtful to say to you or help you. Maybe you're thinking of buying new servers and you wonder whether you should use open source software. . . . IBM has the credibility to offer answers and host this kind of valuable content.

Similarly, GlaxoSmithKline has the credibility to talk about breathing drugs. Lilly has the credibility to talk about diabetic drugs and diabetes. Toyota has the highest satisfaction of car owners in the world; it has the authority to talk about how that happened without giving away any proprietary information.

Companies that are not the largest, highest rated, most successful can take the Avis approach, "how we try harder." Or, like Heeling Sports, show people having a wonderful time with the product. Use the social network to start a dialogue.

Sony Computer Entertainment Europe (SCEE) ran a major online campaign to promote its PlayStation Portable (PSP) handheld game console. Its television ads were designed to drive traffic to the website, which includes information about PSP's game-sharing, online, and Wi-Fi capabilities, as well as details on some of its games and its media player. The ads also point to Sony's Passport To . . . social network travel site (psppassport.com), which promotes Sony's universal media disc travel guides, developed for the PSP in partnership with Lonely Planet.

The site encourages visitors to contribute their own travel stories; Sony posts the best each month as features on the site. And it offers a monthly Q&A competition with chances to win PSPs and travel guides. SCEE is getting conversations going with its target audiences, giving them more reasons to return to the PSP sites, and spotlighting its brand as an authentic source of information and entertainment.[4]

A Slow Build, Not a Quick Transaction

It's tempting to go for the quick transaction: One click on Amazon and you've bought the book. However, what MySpace, FaceBook, and YouTube have taught us about the social network is that you don't have to go for the transaction right away. Create an attractive environment and community; invite people to come, spend some time, meet some people, share some stories, download some content, and you know what . . . you'll probably sell stuff.

It's not just about advertising, it's about links to other things, talking about products, talking about experiences: Did you see the Heelys video? Did you try the virtual racetrack on Pontiac's Second Life site? If people feel comfortable in a social network setting, and even if it is on a company site, they trust you. They are going to share information.

The other lesson from YouTube, MySpace, and FaceBook is that our ideas of privacy are in flux. Some people complain about a lack of privacy, but others are videoing themselves in their bedrooms talking about their so-called lives, disclosing everything about their friends or makeup or bodybuilding. Don't judge it. It's the behavior of the next generation—your customers are doing it, watching it, blogging about it. The real issue is: How do you act in a more social way, rather than a transactional way, to create a brand?

You have to start with some kind of architecture, and I would argue that you have to think about a social network the way you think about a building. The better architect you are, the better social network you will have. Don't confuse this with the software itself. Many companies use proprietary technology but you can also go to companies like Five Across (fiveacross.com), Neighborhood America (neighborhoodamerica.com), and Kick Apps (kickapps.com) for social networking software.

Recently I was on a PBS special about the future of the library. I said libraries have a big future. Almost everybody else on the show disagreed: Who needs a library when you have Google and the Internet? The historian David McCullough and I believe the library has a big future. One of the main reasons I emphasized was the need to be in a special place. When I was a child, there were two very special places I would go—church and library. The library was quiet, orderly, a place of thoughtful contemplation full of people who enjoyed the same experience. The architect had to provide different places for people with different interests: the children's corner, the history area, biography section, fiction shelves, poetry, and so on.

Behavior has not changed that much. The power of creating spaces that people want to come to, want to feel good in, is all part of this movement of social networks and the building of communities. Companies have a right—even a responsibility—to build their own communities and provide spaces for their customers to talk to one another, places for them to learn (using tools like podcasts and microsites). Of course, these communities are places where visitors control what they see, say, do, contribute.

So if you're Pfizer, you want to create a space for a community of physicians, patients, caregivers, insurance companies, and legislators. If you're Whirlpool, you want a community of dealers, distributors, service technicians, suppliers, and regulators. If you're Citibank, you want a community of investors, regulators, customers, media contacts, and financial advisors.

The earlier you embark on the architecture of your own enterprise social network, the better it will become over time as your community tells you what they like, what they don't like, what you see working, what you measure, where you go. I know this is a big revolution. I argue the Internet itself will prove to have more impact than television, radio, or any media that have come before. Social networks will prove to be the most powerful tool for both the social side and the working/business side of online marketing.

What I find fascinating is that we're only in the first generation of social networks. Think how many years the Internet took to become as sophisticated as newspapers, magazines, radio, and television have become and now how fast the digital world is evolving. What are the second and third generations of social networks going to look like? I believe they'll be geared to very narrow interests, not giant sites like MySpace and FaceBook. Many will be enterprise sites with special places to share information with others and watch or download useful or entertaining material—places where visitors are part of the dialogue, not simply passive observers.

Organizing for the Social Web

How do you adapt the traditional marketing department organization to embrace the opportunities inherent in social networks? Even if

CEOs enthusiastically embrace the ideas in this book, they have to obtain the marketing department's cooperation, and that may require a major shuffling of responsibilities. I have noticed some firms organizing to build a community as an integral part of their marketing. This shows up in titles such as "Chief Community Builder" or "Vice President of Communities."

If I were organizing the marketing department to take advantage of the social web, I would first want to be clear about the customer map (which I talked about in Chapter 5) and understand the environment in which my company operates. I would formulate the marketing plan with a long-term campaign perspective in mind. What do we want to accomplish over time in building the communities we envision and what kind of content are we going to need today and tomorrow?

At the top of the marketing pyramid, chief marketing officers (CMOs) will become more like television or movie producers. Instead of having directors of public relations and of advertising, they'll need a director, cinematographer, sound person, set designer, costume designer, makeup artist, editor, key grip, and best boy. Chief marketing officers, who remain responsible for product development and new markets, will have two czars as direct reports: the director of unpaid (social) media and the director of paid media. Ideally, these three managers would work together in planning everything the marketing department will do.

The responsibilities for the director of unpaid media would be community-building, content, customer mapping, analytics and behavior, competitive analysis, competitive landscaping, new media, digital and traditional media relations, and customer care (specifically, customer care content). Also, this executive would be responsible for the organization's search engine optimization, corporate blogs, e-community (or communities), and social networks.

The director of paid media would be responsible for advertising, trade shows, events, loyalty programs, experiential marketing, product placement, and all the promotional materials that the organization has always done. In terms of social networks, the paid media person would be responsible for bringing people to the community, paid opportunities to advertise on television or print or on the Web, direct marketing, and so on. Digital direct marketing and e-mail marketing would be a part of paid media. Search, online banners, buttons, and ads are part of paid media.

I would add third-party relations (analyst communities, partners, etc.) to the marketing department's duties. I'd have somebody in charge of organic and paid search, including responsibility for monitoring all the search engines to make sure the company is properly represented. If the company had plenty of resources, I might have somebody who monitored customer conversations. (If we're allowing customers to post on our site, we do need to screen out obscene, libelous, and inappropriate comments.) What was public relations would now be digital media and community building or new media relations.

Clearly such changes would be a wrench, because advertising in the past was measured by cost per thousand (CPM). While new measurements will include CPM, marketers will now be checking metrics measuring engagement and downloads, for example. How long did a given visitor stay on our site? Who did she interact with? What did she do? Did she download a podcast? Did she watch or download a video? What page did she first view on our site and where did she go when she left the site?

For simplicity, I'd categorize marketing functions in terms of observe, engage, and measure. *Observe* covers all the behavioral and analytics and data about customers, prospects, and competitors. *Engage* covers all the campaigns, the creative, and the community content. *Measure* covers the engagement metrics and the downloads. Some important metrics, as I suggested in the last paragraph, are the number of customers coming to the community and their regular interactions within the community. You'll be able to measure these just as traditional bricks-and-mortar retailers are able to ask people as they walk out of the store, "Did you find what you came for? Were the sales associates helpful? Are you satisfied? Would you recommend our store to your friends and family?"

Similarly, after a customer has been in the digital environment, you could ask: "Did you like it? What would you change? How would you make this better, richer, more rewarding? Would you e-mail a friend about your experience on the site? What did you like most? What did you like least? Is there anything you absolutely hated? What content would you like to see that wasn't there?"

All these questions—and the organization's genuine response to them—can make a richer community, with more experiences, more downloadable content, more sharing of content, more dialogue with and among customers.

And what does all this mean for marketing in the future? What will it be like to live and work in Web 4.0? I have some ideas about that in the next chapter.

CHAPTER 16

Living and Working in Web 4.0

(It's Right Around the Corner)

The Web is no longer new news. I like to say the Web has four phases, and the fourth is right around the corner. The first phase, Web 1.0, ran from about 1989 to 1995, which was the time of website building using HTML.

The second phase, Web 2.0, started with the advent of the browser. Netscape and other browsers enabled people to maneuver around the Web, search more effectively, and do e-commerce more efficiently. We saw the rise of Yahoo and Google. Dot-com companies were hot, hot, hot.

As Web 2.0 started to mature, and even before the dot-com bubble burst, companies had planted the seeds for the social web. Think Amazon, think eBay—both of which promoted a social structure in various ways. Amazon invited users to post product reviews and respond to reviews; eBay had buyers rating sellers. It was (and is) a real community thing.

In the past few years, the social web of Web 3.0 has really taken hold. As I write, we're not only deeply into it, we're moving to a second generation within the social web, more specifically tailored to your interests. Whether you like the Red Sox, want to research diabetes, or collect Star Wars memorabilia, you can connect with your interest on the social web. Companies are just beginning to scatter those seeds now for the next and what I think is the most compelling release of the Web, Web 4.0, the emotive web.

Welcome to the Emotive Web

Web 4.0 is emotive because broadband technology means visual and interactive rich media, and Wi-Fi means the Web is available everywhere—on your laptop, your cell phone, your personal digital assistant. In terms of the individual's control of and demand for words, images, and audio, the emotive web is far beyond television or anything that has ever existed.

In particular, what makes Web 4.0 emotive are the personal and business sensations, the idea that the experiences offer not only emotions—joy, curiosity, disgust, happiness—but also a sense of satisfaction and fulfillment.

Now for the 64 gazillion-dollar question: what does the emotive web mean to marketers?

It means, if nothing else, that we're in a period of transition. "Marketers of all sorts are now being urged to give up the steering wheel to a new breed of consumers who want more control over the ways products are peddled to them," reported Stuart Elliott from the 96th annual conference of the Association of National Advertisers. The group, he wrote in the *New York Times,* heard "one speaker after another describe a need to replace decades worth of top-down marketing tactics with bottom-up grass roots approaches. 'The power is with the consumer,' said A. G. Lafley, chief executive at the Procter &

Gamble. 'Marketers and retailers are scrambling to keep up with her.'"[1] And the social web is where the consumer has the power.

Up to this point, I've laid out what marketers can do to make use of the social web. I'd like to conclude with some suggestions of how the social web in its Web 4.0 phase may affect television, newspapers, and magazines—and what these changes are likely to mean for you and your business.

Where Is Television Going?

I asked my friend Stuart Brotman how he thought the social web would affect television and radio. Stuart is the chairman and CEO of American Television Experience, and holds a concurrent appointment in digital media at Harvard and MIT; he is the past president and CEO of the Museum of Television & Radio.

He thinks that in 10 years, no one will be talking about the Web as a separate medium: "It will be an integral part of media, but it will not be broken out as it is today. We will have a term called 'television,' but television, in fact, may incorporate the Web as a concept. I don't think the Web as a whole is going to subsume television."

Stuart believes that video programming will continue to be delivered through broadcast and cable and fiber optic. Television will continue to be a mass medium, but there will *also* be a mass medium delivered through the Internet. *How* content is delivered will not be important. Remember that most people do not make a distinction between a cable channel and a broadcast channel. When they watch television, they usually don't ponder whether they're watching cable or something else—a situation that has important implications for the social web.

"I think the transmission infrastructure will be transparent to the user," says Stuart, "particularly as the computer becomes an integral part of the home entertainment unit. Whatever comes in on the Internet can immediately get transmitted to a home receiver in a living room, which we now know as a television set." This is already happening: He cites iTV, which is Apple's first foray into transmitting from

210 Making Use of the Four Online Conduit Strategies

the computer directly to the television set. "Clearly we see the beginning of the evolution of content coming off the Internet and not staying on what we know as a computer screen today, but being transmitted to another environment."

For example, think about how people record content off television, manipulate it, transform it (or not), and put it up on YouTube. This traffic—professionals putting out content, amateurs manipulating it and creating their own—is going both ways and will only increase. It's a great time to be an intellectual property lawyer as organizations try to defend their content. As just one example, Japanese television requested that 23,000 clips be taken off YouTube; they were removed within 24 hours.

Other companies may decide for strategic purposes that they want to have their material disseminated as widely as possible, but still within the framework of the intellectual property system. Copyright holders are making these kinds of decisions today and will face even more such decisions in the future.

In-Home Goes Out-of-Home

For a marketer, these changes mean rethinking how they use media. Marketers typically have been organized vertically. They've considered how much to spend on radio . . . how much on broadcast television . . . how much on cable television . . . how much on Internet advertising. Now, Stuart says, "I think a lot of those vertical categories will become more blurred, which poses opportunities and challenges for marketers. It means companies will have more discretion to break down those individual budgets and allocate them. It also means there will be higher risk factors, particularly as attempts are made to develop suitable metrics. How will you be able to measure the effectiveness of a particular ad, with a particular transmission source and a particular receiving device? Measurement will be even more complicated as the lines between in-home usage and out-of-home usage begin to dissolve."

Most marketing messages have been directed out of the home, such as car radios or billboards, or in the home, mainly television sets.

Faster than we can believe, people will own one device that transcends those two marketplaces. They'll carry these devices and be in contact with the Web continuously. Marketers will have to be sensitive to messages for in-home use and out-of-home use simultaneously.

Stuart gives this example: Right now, radio is a short-burst medium organized around 10-, 15-, 20-, 30-, and 60-second ads. But marketing to the social web isn't organized that way. People sit in front of their computers for three or four hours a day linking into various websites, sending and receiving e-mail, and checking archival material. Their involvement is clearly not governed by any particular time frame.

"The out-of-home experience is primarily these bursting messages, which are highly passive," says Stuart. "They're just thrown at you. But in the future, with devices that allow people to take the in-home experience out of home, marketers will have to consider how consumers are managing their time and mobility."

Even now, with mobile media devices being mass marketed in a way that transcends voice telephones, we're trying to get a sense of what people will use them for. Will they use such a device for a short burst of information, or will they use it for long periods of time? If you've seen commuters use their phones on a one-hour train ride instead of reading a newspaper or book or listening to an audio book or CD, you know what I mean. It becomes an hour of experience as opposed to getting the latest headlines, the sports scores, the weather.

Obviously, there's a big difference between being interrupted by a commercial and actively seeking information. If consumers want to know about flat screen television, they want to know as much as possible. There's no comparison between the information they can get from, say, a 30-second Panasonic television commercial and the detailed product specifications and reviews available on the Web. Yet both may be valuable to consumers, for different reasons.

Take Panasonic as an example. Obviously Panasonic should have broad and deep information available on its website, including video demonstrations and specs, reviews, and all the richness of the Web.

Suppose I'm out (with a mobile device) and want to access the Best Buy or Circuit City or *Consumer Reports* site to see the five best-rated flat screen television sets. (This kind of information may or may not be available to the consumer sitting at home or in a Starbucks or on a commuter train.) Once I get the list of five best models, I can visit a store to see each model. I might then go home to think things over before returning to the store or ordering the chosen model online. My point is that there's likely to be interaction between that short piece of information consumers get in the mobile environment and the longer deeper information they get in the stationary environment.

In the near future, for instance, I might have the list of five best-rated flat screen televisions on my cell phone when I visit Best Buy (or another store). I'll be able to transmit that information to my home or office computer so when I turn the computer on or do a Google search, a special marketing system automatically delivers the Panasonic information I'm interested in. And how does the system know I'm interested? Because I was asking about such products when I was in a Best Buy store.

Once you understand the pattern between stationary use (at home or in office) and mobile use, Stuart notes, there are creative strategies you can capitalize on. Rather than developing two different types of marketing messages, you can make them part of a system. The current marketing media system has short bursts of information, which are largely passive, as well as torrents of information, which are largely interactive. "The challenge will be: How do you mesh those two together?" Stuart asks. "Part of the answer will be based on how consumers use their devices and part will be based on how marketers condition consumers to use the devices. These are clearly dynamic processes and marketers can play a role in shaping how those usage patterns get developed."

Where Are Newspapers Going?

I'm not sure whether newspapers, as we know them, will survive. Here are just two quick symptoms of the industry's difficulties:

1. The McClatchy Company bought the *Minneapolis Star Tribune* in 1998 for $1.2 billion. Eight years later, McClatchy sold the paper to a private equity group for just $530 million. As David

Carr wrote in the *New York Times,* "the consolidation of department stores and the flight of classified ads to the Web hurt big metropolitan dailies like the *Star Tribune.* This summer's downturn in overall newspaper advertising landed hard on the paper, with ads off 6.1 percent in the last year from the year before."[2]

2. The *Wall Street Journal* has reduced the size of its pages, put advertising on the front page, and changed its approach to the news. Now the kinds of daily reports and news coverage that everyone carries are on its website, while the physical paper is filled with more analysis and deeper reporting.

I talked to my friend Jerry Swerling about the future of print journalism and the relationship between print and the social web. Jerry has a unique perspective because of his position as professor of professional practice at the Annenberg School for Communication at USC, Los Angeles. He told me: "The problem with print journalism is that they have come to believe that they are in the printing business. The business they're really in is the gathering, interpretation, and distribution of news and information. It's a distribution problem, it's a distribution opportunity, and they're hung-up on the platform."

Jerry asks rhetorically: When you think about the information-intensive age in which we live, what could be more valuable? What greater asset could you have than a large group of well-trained information-gatherers, hunters, distributors? That's a tremendously valuable asset for news organizations to have, yet leveraging that core asset is tricky. How do you distribute it? What is the model? I agree with Jerry when he says, "I don't think anybody has quite figured that one out yet."

What intrigued me was Jerry's example of how print journalism and marketing on the social web may complement one another. "In the automotive section of this morning's *Los Angeles Times,* I noticed that a reporter had written a great review of the latest BMW motorcycle. The review was followed by a couple of lines that said, in effect, 'By the way, not satisfied with what you see on the page, go to such and such a link and you can see the video of her testing the bike. Go along with her.' That's brilliant."

Jerry followed the link and found that readers can comment on the *Times* review and the pros and cons of the BMW bike versus the traditional Triumph or the Harley Davidson bikes. It's a wonderful blend of social networking and journalism. The reporter, he says, "is building a community, in a sense, around her experience and her expertise. And maybe that's the direction in which journalism will have to go: Build a community around your reporters' areas of expertise and create a more personal connection between the reader, the viewer, the consumer."

I can definitely see a role for marketers in this kind of situation. Shouldn't BMW (and Triumph and Harley Davidson and Kawasaki) be part of this discussion? I can see BMW participating in a dialogue to which it would otherwise never have had access. BMW engineers could, for example, explain why they designed the controls or the suspension in a certain way. To be more specific, suppose the reporter's review said, "There was one thing I didn't like about this bike: the transmission isn't as smooth as it could be." A consumer might respond and say, "That's been my problem, too, but it's still a big improvement over the last BMW model." At that point, BMW has a golden opportunity to chime in and say, "Let us tell you why we made that change."

This Is Only the Beginning

You have to understand the landscape to make sense of it, and it's clear that the landscape of the social web is changing almost daily. Volcanoes are erupting (Google, MySpace, YouTube), sinkholes are developing, there are swamps and deserts. Legal and ethical issues such as copyright infringement and privacy are evolving and many areas are, at this writing, grey rather than black or white. The social web is having a major impact, but different industries are going to be affected differently.

Think about how the Web disrupted the music industry and the travel industry, says Judy Strauss, associate professor of marketing at the University of Nevada, Reno. As the whole landscape changed, established firms like Tower Records went out of business and hundreds of travel agents went under.

"The traditional mainstream media industry has this huge disruption," Judy observes. "They're now competing with bloggers for advertising dollars and with the social web for eyeballs," Judy observes. "As users, we want to read whatever is relevant to our particular interests. As a user, I'll go where people are talking about what I'm interested in. In many cases, videos posted by users are more relevant to me than what the media outlets are posting."

Perhaps a constraint on this change is the lack of bandwidth (I know that broadband networks in Korea can be 5 to 10 times faster than America's broadband). Despite the fact that half of all U.S. households have broadband access, significant changes like being able to quickly download high-definition television shows will not become commonplace without more bandwidth.

Judy Strauss stresses that the social web is going to affect different industries in different ways. As you saw earlier in this chapter, it's obviously affecting newspapers and magazines today. It's certainly having an effect on the advertising industry and will probably change the movie industry. (What happens when a million young people are making their own short movies and posting them on YouTube?) Looking ahead, will banking and financial services be the next industry to be disrupted? Or insurance? Or health care?

I don't pretend to have all the answers—but stay tuned because (as I said at the beginning of the book) the social web isn't just a channel or another medium for marketing messages. In effect, it's becoming the closest thing to physical life. This is very important because, whether you're a small company with a chain of restaurants or a giant corporation with a global presence, you're going to have to start talking to customers and prospects as if they were with you in the room.

You'll have to create communities through content, through visual impact, and through conversation, and allow friends and strangers to share their thoughts about your products, your offers, your sales, your weaknesses, your strengths. Through openness, transparency, and truth you can live and thrive on the social web until the Web and marketing disappear.

NOTES

Chapter 1   The Web Is Not a Channel

1. Steve Lohr, "Is Windows Near End of Its Run?" *New York Times,* October 14, 2006, p. C.3.
2. http://publications.mediapost.com/index.cfm?fuseaction=Articles .showArticle&art_aid=45836.
3. Pallavi Gogoi, "Wal-Mart's Jim and Laura: The Real Story," *BusinessWeek Online,* October 8, 2006; Howard Kurtz, "Post Photographer Repays Group for Trip Expenses," *Washington Post,* October 12, 2006, p. C.2; Pallavi Gogoi, "Wal-Mart versus the Blogosphere," *BusinessWeek Online,* October 17, 2006, http://www .businessweek.com.

Chapter 2   Community and Content: The Marketer's New Job

1. Heather Green, "It Takes a Web Village: Private Online Communities Are Providing Special Insights into Customers' Needs," *BusinessWeek,* September 4, 2006, p. 66.
2. Brian Morrissey, "Pontiac Drives into Second Life (IQ)," *Adweek Online,* October 23, 2006, http://www.adweek.com/aw/index.jsp.

Chapter 3   Making the Transition to the Social Web

1. Kate Maddox, "GE Measures Rep in Marketplace," *B to B,* February 13, 2006, p. 27.

2. Chris Gaither, "A Web Contagion," *Los Angeles Times*, August 28, 2005, p. C.1.
3. Hiawatha Bray, "A 'Bold' Step to Fix Ford's Image," *Boston Globe*, September 7, 2006, p. E.1.

Chapter 4   How to Let Customers Say What They Really Think

1. http://www.complaints.com/directory/2006/march/31/18.htm.
2. http://www.my3cents.com/showReview.cgi?id=14668.
3. Bradford Wernle, "Leaked message is not RX for Mazda; Private telecast shows up on Web." *Automotive News*, August 14, 2006, p. 3.
4. Shankar Gupta, "Jeff Jarvis vs. Dell: Blogger's Complaint Becomes Viral Nightmare," http://publications.mediapost.com/index.cfm?fuseaction=Articles.showArticleHomePage&art_aid=33307.
5. Pete Blackshaw, "Lessons from Jeff Jarvis + Dell," http://notetaker.typepad.com/cgm/2005/08/lessons_from_je.html.
6. "Measuring the Influence of Bloggers on Corporate Reputation," December 2005, http://www.onalytica.com/MeasuringBloggerInfluence61205.pdf.
7. "Bloggers FAQ—Online Defamation Law," http://www.eff.org/bloggers/lg/faq-defamation.php.
8. Jonathan Fahey, "Candid Camera: Damage Control in the Age of You Tube," http://www.forbes.com/archive/forbes/2006/1113/124.html.

Chapter 6   Step Two: Recruit Community Members

1. "S-Commerce: Beyond MySpace and YouTube," *Spark*, October 2006 p. 5, www.competeinc.com/research/spark.
2. See note 1, p. 3.
3. "Lego Ambassadors," http://www.lego.com/eng/info/default.asp·age=ambassadors.

Chapter 7   Step Three: Evaluate Online Conduit Strategies

1. Kevin J. Delaney, "Wisdom for the Web: Search-Engine Advertising Is Crucial These Days," *Wall Street Journal*, July 10, 2006, p. R.4.
2. Stefan Stern, "Word on the Blog Says Sun King Rules," *Daily Telegraph*, May 1, 2006, p. 1.

Chapter 8   Step Four: Engage Communities in Conversation

1. Stuart Elliott, "Takes a Licking and Keeps on Floating," *New York Times*, December 1, 2006, p. C.6.
2. Ellen Lee, "Social Sites Becoming Too Much of a Good Thing," *San Francisco Chronicle*, November 2, 2006, http://www.sfgate.com /cgi-bin/article.cgi?f=/c/a/2006/11/02/MNGG3M4KB31.DTL&hw =Social+Sites+Becoming+Too+Much+of+Good+Thing&sn=010 &sc=453.
3. http://www.communispace.com/3_news/press_releases/pr_100406.asp.

Chapter 9   Step Five: Measure the Community's Involvement

1. Rene Algesheimer and Paul M. Dholakia. "Do Customer Communities Pay Off?" *Harvard Business Review*, vol. 84, no. 11, November 2006, p. 26.
2. Diane Brady with David Kiley, "Making Marketing Measure Up," *BusinessWeek*, December 14, 2004, p. 112.
3. Heather Green, "It Takes a Web Village: Private Online Communities Are Providing Special Insights into Customers' Needs," *BusinessWeek*, September 4, 2006, p. 66.
4. http://www.businessweek.com/magazine/content/06_36/b3999076 .htm.
5. Mylene Mangalindan, "E-Commerce: Ad Vantage; New Tools Help Marketers Figure out Which Campaigns Are Worth It," *Wall Street Journal*, June 19, 2006, p. R.11.

Chapter 10   Step Six: Promote Your Community to the World

1. Ellen Byron, "Subject: E-mail Ads Grow Up," *Wall Street Journal*, November 25, 2005, p. B.1.
2. http://getmevisitors.com/works.php.
3. "Baynote Aims to Improve Web Site Navigation," *PC Magazine Online*, June 14, 2006.
4. Stuart Elliott, "Testing Yourself Online and, Maybe, on the Set," http://www.nytimes.com/2006/12/07/technology/07adco.html?_r =1&oref=slogin.
5. Kathleen M. Joyce, "Motivating Out of the Box," *Promo*, November 1, 2006.

Chapter 11   Step Seven: Improve the Community's Benefits

1. The Friendster story is based on Gary Rivlin, "Wallflower at the Web Party," *New York Times*, October 15, 2006, sec. 3, p. 1; Steve Rosenbush, "Why MySpace Is the Hot Place," *BusinessWeek Online*, May 31, 2005; "Friendster Tries for a Comeback," *InternetWeek*, May 19, 2006.
2. "SEO: What Is It? Do I Need it?" http://tcwebsite.com/demo2 /resources/case-studies.
3. "Privacy Policy," http://coachandrea.com/html/privacy_policy.html.
4. Nevertheless, I titled my first book, *The Provocateur: How a New Generation of Leaders Are Building Communities, Not Just Companies* (New York: Crown Business, 2001).
5. John Lawn, "Rememberance of Content past," *Food Management*, April 2006, p. 12.

Chapter 12   The Reputation Aggregator Strategy

1. http://www.nielsen-netratings.com/pr/pr_061120.pdf.
2. Deborah Fallows, "Search Engine Users," Pew Internet & American Life Project, http://www.pewInternet.org/pdfs/PIP_Searchengine _users.pdf.

3. Timothy Daly, "We're Number Two," *Multichannel Merchant*, June 1, 2006.
4. Ralph F. Wilson, "Organic Search versus Paid Search," *Web Marketing Today Free Weekly*, http://www.wilsonweb.com/paid-search /organic-paid.htm.
5. Karen J. Banna, "Honing Your SEM Strategy," *B to B*, July 10, 2006, p. 18.
6. "Paid Search Has Only Slight Edge in Conversion Rates over Organic Search," *WebSideStory News Release*, September 25, 2006, www.websidestory.com; and "Paid Search Not Much Better at Turning Shoppers to Buyers," *InternetWeek*, September 25, 2006.
7. Miguel Helft, "The Retooling of a Search Engine," *New York Times*, December 4, 2006, http://select.nytimes.com/search/restricted /article?res =F70E1FFD345A0C778CDDAB0994DE404482.
8. Mark Roth, "The Thinkers: An Engine that 'Does Search Right,'" *Pittsburgh Post-Gazette*, June 26, 2006, http://www.post-gazette .com/pg/pp06177/701252,stm.

Chapter 13   The Blog Strategy

1. The Oh! Gizmo material is based on Anne Kadet, "Romancing the Bloggers," *SmartMoney*, November 2006, p. 92, and http://www .ohgizmo.com.
2. *Wikipedia*, "blog," http://en.wikipedia.org/wiki (accessed December 20, 2006).
3. "Blogging 'Set to Peak Next Year,'" *BBC News*, December 14, 2006, http://news.bbc.co.uk/2/hi/technology/6178611.stm.
4. Paul Gillin, "New Influencers," http://www.gillin.com/NISurvey .htm.
5. https://extranet.edelman.com/bloggerstudy.
6. Allison Enright, "Brill's Blog Builds Community and Gets It Right," *Marketing News*, December 15, 2005, p. 23.
7. Oliver Ryan, "Blogger in Chief," *Fortune*, November 13, 2006, p. 51.
8. Stefan Stern, "Word on the Blog Says Sun King Rules," http://www .telegraph.co.uk.

9. John Mackey, "Compensation at Whole Foods Market," http://www .wholefoodsmarket.com/cgi-bin/print10pt.cgi?url=/blogs/jm/archives /2006/11 /compensation_at_1.html.
10. http://www.sun.com/aboutsun/media/blogs/policy.html.
11. http://halleyscomment.blogspot.com.
12. http://www.sun.com/rss/podcast.html.

Chapter 14   The E-Community Strategy

1. Jerry Adler, "Fast Chat: Starting a New Slate," *Newsweek*, July 3, 2006, p. 16.
2. Paul, Pamela, "Healthy Babies Need Irony," *New York Times*, December 10, 2006, S.9, p. 2.

Chapter 15   The Social Networks Strategy

1. Jennifer Gill, "Contagious Commercials," *Inc. Magazine*, November 2006, http://www.inc.com/magazine/20061101/handson-marketing.html.
2. "From Early Adoption To Common Practice: A Primer On Online Video Viewing," http://www.online-publishers.org/pdf/opa_online _video_study_mar06.pdf.
3. Robert D. Putnam, *Bowling Alone: The Collapse and Revival of American Community* (New York: Simon & Schuster, 1995), p. vii.
4. "Sony Uses Online to Keep PSP in Spotlight," *New Media Age*, December 21, 2006, p. 2.

Chapter 16   Living and Working in Web 4.0

1. Stuart Elliott, "Letting Consumers Control Marketing: Priceless," *New York Times*, October 9, 2006, p. C.8.
2. David Carr, "The Lonely Newspaper Reader," *New York Times*, January 1, 2007, p. C.1.

INDEX

223